America and the Cold War

ALSO BY RICHARD J. WALTON

The Remnants of Power: The Tragic Last Years of Adlai Stevenson

America
and the Cold War

By RICHARD J. WALTON

★   ★   ★   ★   ★

THE SEABURY PRESS, New York

Grateful acknowledgment is made to the following book publishers and authors for permission to use copyrighted material from the titles listed:

Barnet, Richard J., *Intervention and Revolution*. New York, World, 1968.

Carleton, William G., *The Revolution in American Foreign Policy*. New York, Random House, 1967.

Johnson, Haynes, and Gwertzman, Bernard M., *Fulbright: The Dissenter*. Garden City, N.Y., Doubleday, 1968.

Kennan, George F., *Memoirs 1925–1950*. Boston, Atlantic-Little, Brown and Co. Copyright © 1967 by George F. Kennan.

LaFeber, Walter, *America, Russia and the Cold War, 1945–66*. New York, John Wiley & Sons, 1967.

Lukacs, John, *A New History of the Cold War*. Garden City, N.Y., Doubleday, 1966.

Schlesinger, Arthur M., Jr., *A Thousand Days*. Boston, Houghton Mifflin Company, 1965.

Spanier, John, *American Foreign Policy Since World War II*. New York, Praeger, 1965.

Design by Paula Wiener
Printed in the United States of America

To Richard and Catherine, in the hope that
by the time they read this book
the Cold War will be over.

Contents

America and the Cold War

Prologue

THE Cold War is a curious war, unique to our time. In a sense it is well named, for the two chief protagonists, the United States and Russia, have yet to engage each other in direct military conflict, although they have come terribly close. There is reason to hope they never will.

Still, if the world has thus far avoided nuclear war with its unimaginable consequences, this Cold War has too often been hot. In Korea and Vietnam and in lesser conflicts men have died by the hundreds of thousands. Virtually all these deaths, many of them American, have been suffered far from where the Cold War was born, that tense line dividing Western and Eastern Europe. And the price of the Cold War has been not only death and injury but severe political, social, and economic dislocations the world over, not least in the United States.

There is no one likely to read this book who has not been affected by the Cold War in one way or another, and even if it were somehow to end tomorrow—which is highly im-

1

probable—its effect would be felt for decades. An American need only look at the racial conflict, the disintegrating cities, the disrupted society, to see legacies of the Cold War— legacies that were not even imagined in its early days. And no doubt a Russian could point to unhappy consequences in his own society beyond international tensions and swollen military expenditures. In both nations thought, energy, and money, even moral purpose, have been diverted from impera- tive domestic concerns to the prosecution of this conflict.

It is too early to reach final conclusions about the Cold War. Many American historians have written that the blame for it rests almost entirely with Russia; in recent years in- creasing numbers of "revisionists" have said that the United States is largely to blame. Perhaps, given the nature of the two nations, the Cold War was unavoidable. This book will not attempt to say for sure; its purpose is simply to tell what happened.

It will stress American participation in the Cold War, not only because information about the closed Russian society is difficult to obtain, but more because it is the actions of our own nation that most concern us. The early years of the Cold War will be emphasized; they are less familiar to present-day readers, and it was then that the struggle took its direction and gained the momentum that has carried it to this day.

R.J.W.

1

The Beginning

A DATE can be set for the beginning of the Second World War: September 1, 1939, the day that Hitler's Germany invaded Poland; or, as far as the United States is concerned, December 7, 1941, the day the Japanese bombed Pearl Harbor. But there is no exact date for the beginning of the Cold War.

Some historians have said that it began as early as 1917 with the Communist revolution in Russia, a revolution that met the immediate hostility of Britain, France, and the United States. These nations believed, with good reason, that Lenin and his followers intended for the revolution to sweep through the entire industrial world, upsetting the established order and replacing capitalism with Communism. They can be forgiven, in those chaotic days toward the end of the First World War, for thinking that the Communist movement was a real threat, both immediate and long range. How were they to know—when this strange new phenomenon, part political movement, part religion, was born in turmoil—that it would

3

never achieve power in an industrial nation beyond the reach of the Red Army?

Nor could the new Russian leaders be blamed for their anger against the Western powers who openly interfered in their struggling, uncertain revolution. For the West did try to topple these strange new idealists who believed that their creed was indeed the wave of the future, that their way would bring a better life to the exploited peoples of the industrial nations and the hundreds of millions more in their colonies. Lenin and his followers would not soon forget that British, Japanese, and American soldiers actually occupied parts of Russia during the revolution.

This mutual antagonism existed all through the 20's and 30's. The Western capitalist nations harbored a curious, almost instinctive dread of the alien philosophy of the Soviets, a philosophy born of Marxism, which in various forms and degrees had influenced the workers and intellectuals of Britain, France, Germany, the United States, and all the industrial nations.

Heightening this fear were the crippling depressions that brought shattering misery and social chaos first to Germany and then, after the American "crash" of 1929, to the entire Western world. The social structure of the Western nations seemed on the verge of collapse. To millions, socialism seemed the only answer, but what form and how should it be achieved?

The chaos was exploited in various ways, in various countries, by the Communists, the Socialists, and the Fascists. And somehow, even though the Communists sought only to exploit the original confusion and did not cause it, they were usually held to blame by the threatened ruling groups. This is not to say that the Communists did not adopt violent tactics, for often they did. They believed as an article of faith that capitalism was rotten and corrupt, that it inevitably led to the kind of economic disorder they were then trying to exploit, and that any means was justified to achieve the end of pulling down the decayed structure and replacing it with Communism.

But it would take a separate book to sort out the political and economic mess of the 20's and 30's. The Nazis under Hitler, the Fascists under Mussolini, and other right-wing groups were also trying to exploit the disorder, and their tactics were often no less violent than the Communists'. Then there were democratic Socialists, and social reformers of various leftist degrees, and progressives and conservatives and monarchists—a bewildering profusion of political parties, engaged in equally bewildering and constantly shifting alliances.

During all this time the various Western governments were making frantic but not always successful efforts to set their economic and political houses in order and to carry on the complex diplomacy of the time. When Hitler finally triumphed amidst the ruins of the Weimar Republic in 1933, this diplomatic dance took on an even wilder aspect. Britain and France could have crushed the German dictator in his earliest days, but they were preoccupied with their domestic problems and could not bring themselves to take united action even when Hitler's menace became obvious to all. And the United States, disillusioned by events that followed the war "to save Democracy," turned its back on Europe and refused to join the League of Nations founded by its President, Woodrow Wilson.

Further complicating the situation were the stories filtering
out of Soviet Russia about the show trials, the purges of the
late 30's in which thousands, perhaps millions of Russians
were imprisoned and often killed for "betraying" Marxism-
Leninism by some real or imagined or fabricated offense,
usually the latter two. This sullen and dark nation became a
nightmare land where crimes beyond imagination were committed by a stern ruler, Josef Stalin, to whom suspicion or
even the possibility of suspicion were enough to merit the
death sentence. As the truth of these stories became apparent, it began to discredit Russia even with many who had
been its best friends abroad. Millions still shared the goals of
Communism as originally conceived, but could not counte-
nance its means as practiced in Russia.

As the 30's neared their end, Britain and France continued
their appeasement of Hitler. Stalin, long fearful of the Third
Reich—the Nazis and Communists had been mortal enemies
in Germany—evidently came to believe that Britain and
France were conspiring with Hitler so he would be free to
attack Russia. Then when Hitler and Stalin shocked the
world with their nonaggression pact in 1939, Britain and
France felt that Stalin had made a deal at their expense so
that Hitler could attack them.

This was not a noble time for European diplomacy. Hitler's
eventual foes to the east and west could have combined to
stop him at any time almost to the very end. But Britain and
France on one hand, and Russia on the other, could not bring
themselves to work together for their mutual safety. So Hitler,
playing on what can only be called timidity and stupidity,
turned first on the West and then on the East, and came
within a trice of defeating them both.

Thus, when what came to be called the Grand Alliance was formed in 1942, it was hardly a natural alliance. Winston Churchill, the indomitable wartime Prime Minister of Britain, and Josef Stalin, the shrewd but brutal tyrant, were more natural enemies than allies. And Franklin D. Roosevelt, the senior member of the triumvirate, had reservations about both his British and Russian allies. It was not surprising, then, that even the struggle against a common enemy, Hitler's Germany, could not completely submerge natural tensions.

Despite the enormity of American aid (some $9½ billion in lend-lease, a much greater sum in those pre-inflationary days than it seems now), despite the incredible courage of British and American sailors in carrying war matériel to Murmansk through icy seas infested with German U-boats and warships while under constant pounding of the Luftwaffe, despite the almost nonstop bombing of German war plants, despite the Anglo-American invasions of North Africa and Italy, Stalin constantly accused his allies of deliberately delaying the opening of a second front in Western Europe that would take pressure off Russian armies.

His feelings can perhaps be understood, for seldom in the history of warfare have armies been so cruelly punished. Time and time again it seemed as if Russian resistance must collapse under the incredible battering of the German armies and air fleets. Only courage of the most magnificent sort held the Germans off at Stalingrad in 1943. And even though the American and British leaders did not consider allowing Russia to fall, there were those in both countries who counseled before and during the war that the best thing the West could do would be to let Russia and Germany fight each other to death. Stalin no doubt heard of such counsel and, fearing the imminent collapse of the Russian armies, it was only natural for him to be increasingly suspicious of Western motives.

When the Allies landed on the beaches at Normandy, France, on D-Day, June 6, 1944, these tensions abated considerably. But even as American and British armies fought their way across France, Belgium, and eventually Germany, Stalin never forgot that his nation, devastated as it was, continued to bear the major burden of the land war in Europe. Most Americans naturally, through movies and television and books, have focused almost exclusively on the advance of American forces across Western Europe. Yet in the last months of the war, for every one German division that faced General Dwight D. Eisenhower, three battled the advancing Russians.

On April 25, 1945, the victorious Americans met the victorious Russians in the middle of Europe, along the banks of the Elbe River near the German town of Torgau. It was a joyous meeting and the soldiers of both armies—few, if any, able to speak the language of the other—celebrated with songs and drink late into the night. At that moment it seemed that the hopes for lasting peace could come true, that the two most powerful nations in the world, the United States and Russia, could, standing together, prevent any threat to peace for decades to come. And on May 8, when President Harry S. Truman and Prime Minister Winston Churchill proclaimed the end of the European war, and the United Nations was approaching birth in San Francisco, these hopes must have seemed at last within reach. For the Asian war, too, was almost over.

On August 6 the United States dropped an atomic bomb on

Hiroshima, destroying more than half the city and killing a quarter or more of its 344,000 people. It was the cataclysmic start of a new and frightening era.

Truman's decision to drop the bomb on Hiroshima, and on Nagasaki three days later, has been a subject of controversy ever since. Did any nation, whatever the cause, have the right to use such a weapon? Or did Truman act correctly, convinced as he was that it would end the war almost immediately and thus spare the hundreds of thousands of lives that military leaders believed would be lost in a conventional conquest of the fiercely defended Japanese homeland? Although the debate continues, with no generally accepted conclusion in sight, there is little doubt that the use of the atomic bomb, together perhaps with the entry of Russia into the Pacific war, did cause the Japanese to surrender only days later, on August 14.

Many Americans who have supported a hard line in the Cold War have argued that Russia came into the war only to get a share of the spoils of victory. They point to the date when the Russian offensive in Manchuria began, August 8, two days after Hiroshima, as proof that Russia entered only when the war was obviously all but over. But the fact is that Russia had committed itself to enter the war months before at the Yalta Conference in the Russian Crimea. There, between February 3 and 11, 1945, Roosevelt, Churchill, and Stalin agreed, among other things, that Russia would join in the Pacific war three months after the end of the European war. This Russia did, exactly to the day.

Hard-liners have also argued that Roosevelt and Churchill should never have asked Stalin to join the war against Japan, that because of atomic weapons, Russian help was not needed in conquering the Japanese, and that its participation would only mean an increase of Russian influence in Asia. But these critics argue with hindsight. The Americans did not successfully test the first atomic bomb at Alamogordo, New Mexico, until July 16. Thus in February, Anglo-American military commanders had to plan on finishing the war against Japan by conventional means, and they were convinced that Russian participation would enormously reduce the number of British and, primarily, American casualties.

Whatever the subsequent controversies, the Second World War, the bloodiest ever fought by man, came to an end on August 14, 1945, nearly six years after it began. The world, amidst its rejoicing, swore that it would never happen again, that the newly created United Nations, as stated in the Preamble to its Charter, would indeed ". . . save succeeding generations from the scourge of war, which twice in our lifetime has brought untold sorrow to mankind. . . ."

What kind of a world was there on that joyous day? It was a world profoundly changed. The British Empire, for centuries the most powerful political and economic force in the world, was exhausted and soon would begin to disintegrate, reducing mighty Britain to a second-rate power. The French Empire, too, was on the verge of collapse, although a bloody decade was to elapse before it would surrender its grip on its last African colonies and turn over to America its troubles in Indochina. All of Europe was prostrate, and Germany, the ambitious nation whose Hitler had started it all, lay in ruins. Japan, conqueror of almost all Asia, was crushed. Even Russia, now the mightiest nation in Europe, lay devastated, crippled by the German armies and Luftwaffe. Its losses were almost beyond imagination: a quarter of its capital equipment, 1700 towns, 70,000 villages, nearly 100,000 collective farms destroyed and, difficult to comprehend, more than twenty million dead.[1] (See notes at back of book following the Epilogue.) No nation in history had ever suffered more cruelly in war.

And the United States? It stood alone, unchallenged as the world's supreme power. Although it too suffered severe losses —more than 400,000 killed—they were small compared to those of the other participants and its civilian population had been spared the destruction visited on most of Europe and Asia and North Africa. Its economy was untouched by the war and indeed was infinitely stronger because of it. And most significant of all, only America had The Bomb.

How then did the Cold War begin so soon after the victory that saw the United States and Russia comrades-in-arms? There is no shortage of theories. They range widely. On one extreme there is the belief that Stalin intended to extend Communism forcibly not only to the Eastern European nations that lay uneasily beneath his conquering armies but to all of Western Europe, exhausted by war, shattered and defenseless before Russian might. But this theory, believed as an article of faith by many Americans and some Western Europeans, does not seem to hold up to close analysis. To be sure, Russia did clamp a brutal grip on the Eastern European countries along its border. Yet there has never been any real evidence that it wanted to extend its *direct* control into Western Europe, although it would probably have been happy indeed to see Communist parties assume power in France and Italy where they were already strong.

Even if there can be no certain knowledge of Stalin's intentions, it is quite clear that the last thing Russia wanted was another war. Further, any extension of its control into Western Europe would have sorely overtaxed its depleted strength. And Stalin had always been a cautious man; he was not one to overlook America's unchallengeable might, particularly the atomic bomb.

No, that theory seems too extreme, even though it may well be true that there was a terrible fear in Western Europe and among American officials that the Russians were contemplating a sweep to the English Channel. This fear, even if it had no actual basis in fact, was itself real and certain to influence Western behavior.

On the other extreme is the belief that America in 1945 felt itself empowered and uniquely equipped to remake the world in its image, felt that Communism was a mortal threat and that it had to be quarantined by any means—political, economic, and, if need be, military. A corollary to this is the belief that America saw the prostrate world as a unique opportunity for American business and industry. There may be some element of truth to this theory as there is to that of Communist conquest, but each is too pat, seems to be tailored to fit an ideology rather than the confused circumstances of the first months and years after the war.

Perhaps more valid is the view that only the mortal peril of Hitler could have made allies of nations so profoundly different in philosophy and structure as the United States and Russia. The desperate need to resist and then conquer German and Japanese imperialism submerged these differences, but once the necessity to cooperate was gone, they inevitably surfaced. Russia was deeply suspicious of the West, feared a resurgence of its mortal enemy, Germany, and was convinced that America was beginning a hostile encirclement. The United States, on the other hand, was revulsed by the Russian takeover of Eastern Europe and convinced that it foreshadowed a Communist expansion into the whole of Europe that must be stopped at all costs. For if Russia were to succeed, American security—even its survival—would be imperiled.[2]

It was thus that the two giants, one relatively stronger than it would ever be again, the other severely weakened but certain to gain strength, regarded one another.

But if blame cannot be apportioned, the facts may be examined. What did these two great nations want? Stalin's first need was to rebuild his shattered nation. For this he demanded and got huge reparations from Germany. He also wanted to protect the physical security of Russia. Since there were no natural defenses, he chose the traditional Russian defense, space. And since his conquering armies occupied Poland, Czechoslovakia, Hungary, Rumania, Bulgaria, and eastern Germany, he simply took them, blandly telling the West that since he hadn't interfered with their plans in Belgium, the Netherlands, and Italy, they should leave him alone in areas of strategic concern to Russia. This also fitted in with Communist ideology, that it should spread from its birthplace.

As for the United States, its goals were even more difficult to define. But despite criticism by some historians in the late 60's, there is no reason to doubt the genuineness of America's interest at the end of the war in establishing conditions of lasting peace. It took no territory, although no nation could have resisted it. Indeed, the United States dismantled its victorious armies at a rate that many found alarming. President Truman reduced the army in Europe from 3.5 million to half a million in less than ten months, partly in response to pressure "to get the boys home," partly to reduce military spending. He was confident that American political and economic strength, and its monopoly of the atom bomb, were sufficient defenses.

America's concern in playing the major role in founding the United Nations, its concern for the peoples behind what Churchill soon labeled the "Iron Curtain," its concern for the peoples of Western Europe—all these were genuine. But just as the Communists in Moscow viewed the world in a distinct way, so did the American government. It believed the world should exist under terms of Western, free-enterprise democracy, and employed its enormous political and economic strength to that end.

Just after Japan's surrender, this is the way the American Secretary of State James F. Byrnes viewed the world:

"Our international policies and our domestic policies are inseparable," he began. "Our foreign relations inevitably affect employment in the United States. Prosperity and depression in the United States just as inevitably affect our relations with the other nations of the world." Byrnes expressed his "firm conviction that a durable peace cannot be built on an economic foundation of exclusive blocs . . . and economic warfare. . . . [A liberal trading system] imposes special responsibilities upon those who occupy a dominant position in world trade. Such is the position of the United States." In announcing the American intention to reorder the world, he uttered a warning as well as a policy assumption: "In many countries throughout the world our political and economic creed is in conflict with ideologies which reject both of these principles. To the extent that we are able to manage our domestic affairs successfully, we shall win converts to our creed in every land." [3]

In short, the United States was determined to establish the economic ground rules for world trade, trade that it knew it could not help but dominate for years to come.

It is with this background that we examine the actual events of what within two years, in a series of newspaper columns by Walter Lippmann, would be called the Cold War.

2
Growing Tensions

As soon as his armies marched into Eastern Europe, Stalin made it plain—and American and British entreaties could not move him an inch—that he was going to establish those countries as pro-Soviet buffer states between Russia and the country which had twice invaded it within twenty-five years, Germany. Thus, the Iron Curtain descended, but it did not descend all at once. It took nearly three years to clank completely shut with the Communist takeover in Czechoslovakia in 1948. And it has been argued by some, among them President Tito of Yugoslavia, that the Iron Curtain was, at least in part, a Russian response to American moves.[1]

Perhaps that is so, but there seems little doubt that Stalin had always intended to dominate those nations along Russia's borders—indeed, this was a Russian imperial ambition that long predated the revolution—although, of course, the extent and terms of that domination may have been influenced by American actions. The blunt fact is that none of

16

Russia's East European neighbors have known genuine national freedom since the Red Army stormed across their frontiers toward the end of the war. Stalin, however, did permit free elections in the Soviet zone of Austria (the Communists were badly beaten) and he did permit Finland, which was not so strategically placed, to go its own way.

The Americans and the British protested bitterly that Stalin had broken the promise he'd given at Yalta that the Eastern European nations were to have free elections. The Russians blandly replied that they had held free elections, although in most cases, by any normal Western standards, that was simply untrue. But equally untrue—and there always seem to be several sides in discussing the Cold War—are the allegations often made by American hard-line anti-Communists that the West "sold out" Poland and the other Eastern European nations. The United States and Britain did not sell out Eastern European countries for the simple reason that they were not theirs to sell. These countries were held by the Red Army, and the West, in trying to establish some semblance of self-determination in Eastern Europe, was playing with a very weak hand.

The United States was deeply disturbed by Stalin's unyielding stand, and Stalin was angered by what he considered Western interference in Russia's legitimate sphere of influence. Nonetheless, there was no immediate break, for there were still remnants of the feeling of alliance, particularly with some American leaders, and Stalin hoped to receive from the United States some of the massive economic aid necessary to rebuild his nation.

If Eastern Europe was a great source of tension, though, Germany was perhaps an even greater one. Indeed, from the beginning of the Cold War to the present, Germany, more than any other single issue, has caused tension, and often much more than that, between the United States and Russia. At first, the United States and Britain wanted "Germany politically whole and, after destroying her war-making potential, [to] restore industry to a self-supporting level; the Allies would thus not have to expend their own resources to keep Germany alive. The Soviets, supported in large part by the French, preferred a politically divided, economically weakened Germany. Stalin's tactics included demands for huge reparations to be taken out of the German industrial complex." [2]

After difficult negotiations, Russia agreed to accept 25 per cent of German capital equipment from the three Western zones (controlled separately by the United States, Britain, and France) and to have a free hand in its own zone. This was, of course, to make up for the enormous losses in Russia caused by the Germans. Perhaps predictably, East and West each imposed its own system on its section of Germany. The Russians broke up the great Prussian estates, took over industry, and forced Communist control on local political parties. The United States increased German industrial production, at least in part to make West Germany attractive to American investors. And it began to encourage the emergence of democratic but anti-Communist and pro-Western political parties.

Particularly on the German question but on others as well, the West and Russia often shifted position, not infrequently switching sides. One such changing position was the American view on how to use the atomic bomb in its relationship with Russia. In mid-1945 Secretary of War Henry Stimson hoped that the bomb would result in "less barbarous relations with the Russians," and he believed world peace was unobtainable until "Russia's secret police state" opened itself up in the nature of Western democracies.[3] But he soon suggested a shift in tactics. Just before leaving office, he sent a memorandum to President Truman in which he predicted "that it would not be possible to use our possession of the atomic bomb as a lever to produce the change" wanted in Eastern Europe. And Stimson warned Truman that if Soviet-American negotiations continued with "this weapon rather ostentatiously on our hip, their suspicions and their distrust of our purposes and motives will increase." He went on to suggest direct bilateral talks with the Soviets to formulate control of atomic energy and reach agreement on a general peace settlement.

There seems little doubt that Stimson was right. Although the Russians must have had a healthy respect for the A-bomb, they were successful in acting as if it didn't greatly concern them. Certainly the bomb did not for a moment deter them in clamping down the Iron Curtain. And as eager as the Russians must have been to see some limitation put on America's use of its nuclear monopoly, the two sides were unable to reach any agreement on nuclear weapons until long after Russia itself possessed them.

Since direct talks failed to get Stalin to relax his iron grip on Eastern Europe, the United States tried economic pressure. Russia desperately needed capital for reconstruction. In fact, in January of 1945 Stalin had asked the United States for a $6 billion loan. But the State Department refused to discuss the matter until, as Ambassador Averell Harriman told Stalin, Russia adopted a more acceptable policy in

Europe. Then in May, after the surrender of Germany, Truman abruptly cut off lend-lease aid to Russia.

Nevertheless, Stalin did not immediately dismiss the possibility of aid from his American allies. He asked again, this time for $1 billion. No action was taken on the request until several months later after an unsuccessful foreign ministers' meeting in December. Then, in March 1946, the United States agreed to consider the loan if Russia would join the International Bank for Reconstruction and Development (World Bank) and the International Monetary Fund. Joining would require that Russia, traditionally a secretive and suspicious nation, open its books to the international agencies which, of course, were dominated by the United States, the only nation with much money to lend. Less than two weeks later, March 13, Russia announced a Five-Year Plan to rebuild heavy industry and to ensure "the technical and economic independence of the Soviet Union." And two days after that Stalin turned down the American offer.

Here as elsewhere in the early days of the Cold War, it is impossible to determine which action was a cause and which an effect. Was the tough American position a result of Soviet expansion in Eastern Europe, or did it encourage such expansion, or was there a continuous interaction? One eminent historian of the Cold War, John Lukacs, has no doubts. He says, "Stalin, not Truman, was the principal architect of the Iron Curtain and the Cold War." But he also goes on to say, "A new and world-wide American expansion was beginning; and whether the accumulating evidence of Stalin's brutalities and ambitions between 1945 and 1947 alone caused this reaction or merely accelerated its development is not important—at least not here." [4]

Although American interest was centered on Europe, in late 1945 it made a quick foray to China. There was always the fear that China's millions might be added to the Russian Empire. It was fashionable then to assume, and the assumption was slow to vanish even in the face of unmistakable evidence to the contrary, that any country with a Communist government was necessarily subservient to Moscow. But even in 1945, four years before the Communists achieved power in China, there was clear evidence of tension between Mao Tsetung, the Chinese Communist leader, and Stalin.

On August 14, the very day that Japan surrendered, Russia signed a Treaty of Friendship and Alliance with Chiang Kai-shek, the anti-Communist ruler of China. This could not have been welcomed by Mao. Clearly Stalin was not at all sure the Communists were going to win in China. For ideological reasons he no doubt wanted the Communists to triumph, but the cautious old tyrant was always a nationalist first and the emergence of another Communist Rome in Peking must have been a source of some worry. With a large and potentially powerful neighbor, with a common frontier thousands of miles long, it is quite conceivable that he was tempted by the idea that a divided China would be a more comfortable neighbor than a united China, even a Communist one. Also by the treaty Stalin gained recognition of his *de facto* control of Outer Mongolia, sharing of the port facilities of Dairen, the acquisition of Port Arthur as a naval base, and, most important, joint ownership in the Manchurian Railway, a many-sided business and industrial venture that had great influence in that rich province.[5]

The Americans were concerned that China might go Communist. Yet with a war just over, they did not want to take on the imposing, perhaps impossible job of cementing the Chiang Kai-shek regime, for even then it was apparent that it was incompetent and corrupt. So Truman sent to China General George C. Marshall, the superb strategist who had presided from Washington over the entire Allied war effort. His job was no less than to establish a coalition government headed by Chiang that would include the Communists of Mao, Chiang's mortal foe. This was a task beyond even General Marshall. He succeeded by mid-February 1946 in working out a tentative settlement that included a cease-fire between the Nationalists and the Communists. But two months later the agreement had become unstuck. The Communists were difficult and, perhaps more important, Chiang, whose forces outnumbered the Communists five to one, was confident that he could defeat them on the battlefield—and that Washington had no choice but to give him all the help he needed to do so. Chiang, however, was terribly wrong, as Mao was to prove in only four years.

Important as China was, for Washington the main arena was still Europe. There, in 1946, the impetus toward a lasting Cold War might have been stopped, but neither the United States nor Russia seemed able to take the necessary action.

In February, Stalin made a tough speech calling on the Russians to make enormous sacrifices to prepare themselves for the struggle with the capitalists. Then, on March 5, after an introduction by President Truman, Winston Churchill made his famous Iron Curtain speech. He told the audience at Westminster College in Fulton, Missouri, that "from Stettin in the Baltic to Trieste in the Adriatic, an iron curtain has descended across the continent," allowing "police governments" to rule Eastern Europe. Churchill said that although the Soviets did not want war, "what they desire is the fruits of war and the indefinite expansion of their power and doctrines." [6]

More important than contributing an enduring phrase to our language, Churchill called for the creation by the Americans and the British, with the support of atomic weapons, of "a unity in Europe from which no nation should be permanently outcast." This "fraternal association of the English-speaking peoples" would operate under the principles of the United Nations but not within it.

Stalin was not long in responding. Within a few days he accused Churchill and his "friends" in the United States of holding a Hitler-like "racial theory" that the English-speaking nations "should rule over the remaining nations of the world." And he termed the Churchill plan "a call to war with the Soviet Union." Stalin defended the basis of Russian occupation of Eastern Europe by recalling that twice in the recent past Germany had invaded Russia through those countries when ruled by "governments inimical to the Soviet Union." Then Stalin challenged Churchill by declaring that Communism, despite the Briton's belief, was "normal" in Europe, indeed more than normal; it was "the law of historical development."

Clearly Churchill had alarmed Stalin and just as clearly Stalin alarmed the West, particularly when he immediately embarked on a series of decisive actions. In addition to turning down the offer (with strings attached) of a $1 billion American loan, he initiated a policy in Iran that caused the first direct confrontation with the United States. Stalin refused to pull his troops out of Iran by the March 8 deadline, even though the British and Americans had already withdrawn theirs sent during the war. Stalin obviously wanted to establish Russian influence in the neighboring kingdom. But he must have decided that the United States was not bluffing when it and Britain sent stiff notes; for Russia in late March announced that it would withdraw its troops. During March, Russian forces in Manchuria also arranged that Chinese Communist troops would get control of surrendered Japanese arms, yet, according to Stalin's ambivalent policy, turned over Manchurian cities to Nationalist garrisons.

Perhaps most significant of these March decisions was the change in Russian policy toward reparations from the Soviet zone of Germany. At first the Russians stripped East Germany of its manufacturing equipment and sent it to Russia to replace that destroyed by the Germans, but early in 1946 the Russians decided it would be better to use East German equipment and labor right on the spot and send the manufactures to Russia. This, of course, implied an intention to stay, as did the Communization of the section and the deification of Stalin.

Then, in April of that year, Stalin finally rejected a treaty calling for a unified and demilitarized Germany which had been proposed by U.S. Secretary Byrnes in late 1945. (Later, Russia and the United States would switch positions.) Not only was Stalin fearful of a reunited Germany, but he had decided to use East Germany as a factory for the reconstruction of Russia. A few days later, on May 3, the United States reacted. General Lucius Clay, the American commander in Germany, told the Russians, despite the earlier agreement, that they could remove no more German capital equipment from the Western zones. Thus, the positions of both sides hardened on what was then, and still is, the key to a European settlement: Germany.

Another Russian-American clash occurred at the United Nations when on June 14 Bernard Baruch presented the U.S. plan for the international control of atomic energy. The Baruch Plan gave, in effect, most of the control to the United States. This was hardly surprising, for it is unlikely that any nation would willingly surrender its monopoly on a weapon that gave it unquestioned military superiority over the whole world. Nor was it surprising that after months of talks the Russians, who wanted the wholly unrealistic destruction of all (meaning American) atomic weapons, rejected the American plan in October.

Still another sign of the growing Russian-American hostility was a speech by Secretary Byrnes in Stuttgart, Germany, on September 6. For the first time an American official said publicly what had been developing in U.S. foreign policy for months: that the United States would not recognize as the German-Polish border the line along the Oder-Neisse Rivers (a matter of grave concern to the Poles and the Russians); that the German economy would have to be expanded so that the nation was self-sustaining; that Germany had to be given the primary responsibility for managing its own affairs (this alarmed the Russians—and the French); and, no less important, that American troops were in Europe to stay.

A speech by another leading member of the Truman Administration demonstrated how far the Cold War had developed by late 1946. The speaker was Henry Wallace, an imaginative Secretary of Agriculture in the early days of Roosevelt's New Deal, Vice President from 1941 to 1945, and Secretary of Commerce in 1945–46. On September 12, 1946,

Wallace, in a speech cleared by Truman himself, proclaimed the necessity of a political understanding between the United States and Russia. In clearing the speech Truman was obviously following the practice of many Presidents, trying to juggle the policies of differing factions of his party. The reaction of the other faction was instantaneous. Secretary Byrnes and Senator Arthur Vandenberg, the leading Republican on foreign policy matters and one whose cooperation was essential to a bipartisan foreign policy, were outraged. From Paris where they were negotiating with the Russians, they demanded that Truman fire Wallace. He did a week later.

According to the historian Walter LaFeber:

The vigor of this reaction to Wallace's speech measured the distance American policy had moved since the close of World War II. Wallace was essentially pleading for a renewal of the Administration's invitation of 1945 to the war-decimated Russian economy to join a friendly game of economic competition with the American industrial mammoth and to play the game according to American rules. By mid-1946, Truman and Byrnes had moved far beyond this. They now assumed that the Russians would not accept such rules but would cooperate only when faced with the threat of superior military force. Wallace argued that such a threat would only result in expansive military establishments with less security and prosperity on both sides.[7]

Henry Wallace was not alone in such criticism. Many liberal Democrats shared it, among them such notables as Henry Morgenthau, Jr. and Harold Ickes, great figures of the Roosevelt years. This dissent grew into a political movement out of which emerged the Progressive party which ran Wallace for President in 1948. He received just a little over a million votes.

Partly because he advocated what even then was an un-popular cause, and partly because he received electoral sup-port from the American Communists, Wallace became known as a radical, although he was no such thing. He was a New Deal reformer with distinctly conservative views on some matters. In any case, it is interesting to speculate on what might have happened if Roosevelt had not eased Wal-lace out as the Vice Presidential candidate in 1944, for if he hadn't, Wallace and not Truman would have become Presi-dent in 1945.

There were other important developments in late 1946. Behind Churchill's Iron Curtain, Soviet power removed opposition parties so that the Communists could win safe majorities in Rumania in November and in Poland in January 1947. And there was a brief but significant con-frontation with the United States over Turkey.

Although forced out of Iran by the tough American stand, Stalin had other aspirations in that area, this time the age-old Russian dream of an opening through the Dardanelles Straits into the Mediterranean. As early as June 1945, Russia had made demands on Turkey. It pressured Turkey to cede several districts along the frontier, to revise the Montreux Convention concerning the Dardanelles in favor of joint Russian-Turkish administration, to conclude a treaty with Russia that would put Turkey into a satellite status, and to lease land and naval bases on the Straits for its "joint defense."

These demands were renewed in August 1946, but the Turks mobilized their army, the United States moved a task force into the Mediterranean and, a few days later, sent the Russians a stiff note rejecting their demands. Again the Russians had probed for a weakness, and again when they found resistance they pulled back. But it should be carefully noted that these tough but cautious probes were not Communist in nature but Russian, for Russia long before Communism had sought access to the Mediterranean and the Middle East.

In the final month of 1946 the United States and Britain, over the objections of France and Russia, economically joined their two German zones. This was clearly another step toward the integration of these zones into the Western economy and another blow for the Soviet Union which had as a basic goal keeping Germany out of the Western camp.

With American attention so riveted on Europe, what was happening in Asia, and particularly in Indochina, hardly seemed important, even though it was to change the course of American history. The French in Indochina refused to make any substantial concessions to the Vietminh nationalists seeking eventual independence. Then, in late 1946, an armed rebellion broke out, led by a Vietnamese Communist virtually unknown elsewhere in the world: Ho Chi Minh.

3

The Point of No Return

ALTHOUGH both the United States and Russia had taken steps to escalate the Cold War in 1945 and 1946, it had not yet frozen solid. It is impossible to know exactly what the Soviet position was at the time, but the United States had not quite made up its mind. It was still wavering at the end of 1946 between two extreme positions, Churchill's and Wallace's.

Churchill argued that the Soviet Union had already adopted an expansionist policy and that Britain and America had to take strong countermeasures, while Wallace complained that Churchill's militant stance was to blame for Russian hostility. But in early 1947 the pendulum swung strongly in Churchill's favor and the course of world history was set for decades to come.

What was the situation as that fateful year began? The Iron Curtain had begun to ring down over Eastern Europe, angering the West, whose response in turn angered Stalin. This is how the historian John Lukacs saw it:

Thus an amused historian may say that the first few years, and perhaps even the first decade (I wrote this first in 1950) of the Russian-American crisis over Europe might have been due to a fundamental, mutual misunderstanding: Washington presupposing that the immediate Russian aim was to upset and conquer Western Europe, Moscow presupposing that the American aim was to upset and reconquer Eastern Europe—and that both presuppositions were wrong.[1]

About Russian thinking in those early years—or any years since—we can only speculate. But we do know that as far as the Americans were concerned, the moment for decision came on February 21, 1947. On that day the British First Secretary in Washington had the melancholy task of admitting that the United Kingdom was no longer a great power. In two separate notes His Majesty's Government informed the United States that it could not continue to carry out its traditional responsibilities in Greece and Turkey. Greece, fighting a civil war against Greek Communists, and Turkey, under constant Russian pressure, needed $250 million in military aid, and Britain, whose economy was on the verge of collapse, no longer could carry the burden.

The United States was being asked to assume Britain's ancient role as world policeman. "Now, all of a sudden," political analyst John Spanier relates, "there was no one to protect the United States but the United States itself; no one stood between this country and the present threat to its security." [2] This was the view of Truman and most of his top advisers. They saw Communism turning the flank of Europe and spilling through the Middle East and North Africa.

A few days later Harry S. Truman made the most important speech of his career. At one o'clock on Wednesday,

March 12, he stepped to the rostrum in the House of Representatives to address a joint session of Congress. Recommending immediate action, he also emphasized that he wanted the whole world to know "what the position of the United States was in the face of the new totalitarian challenge." This policy, he said, would be "the turning point" in American foreign policy. Now, according to Truman, the security of the United States was involved "wherever aggression, direct or indirect, threatened the peace." And then the President went on to use one sentence that has been the key to American foreign policy for more than twenty years: "I believe that it must be the policy of the United States to support free peoples who are resisting attempted subjugation by armed minorities or by outside pressures." [3]

Truman, of course, had to await Congressional approval, but while waiting he did what he could to encourage the Greek government. "Secretary [of the Navy James] Forrestal, on my instructions, dispatched the aircraft carrier *Leyte* and nine other vessels on a visit to Greece as a token of our intention, hoping to persuade the British to stay on, at least until our aid to Greece became effective." [4]

This policy decision, taken by Truman in the waning days of February and the first days of March 1947, and later called the Truman Doctrine, deserves the most careful examination. For it led almost inevitably to the subsequent American actions in Korea, Iran, Guatemala, Cuba, the Dominican Republic, and Vietnam. And, because Soviet moves were often a reaction to American moves, and vice versa, it led to many Russian actions as well.

To understand the situation, we need to go back a little in time. The immediate reason given to justify the Doctrine was the imminent fall of Greece. After the Nazi invasion of Greece in 1941, several indigenous underground resistance movements had sprung up. ELAS, led by Greek Communists, was the largest and best organized, despite an initial lack of assistance from other Communist groups. A year or so after the resistance began, a Soviet military mission visited ELAS headquarters in the mountains and dismissed the guerrillas as "just a rabble of armed men, not worth supporting." And Bulgarian guerrillas, operating just across the border with Russian aid, also refused to send aid.

When the Germans and Italians began to pull out in 1944, the rival Greek guerrilla groups began a struggle for control of the country, with the British supporting the smaller group led by conservative army officers and installing a pro-monarchist government in Athens.

Gradually, the Greek Communists took over most of the country, using arms captured from the retreating Axis armies. They were successful in this, even though Stalin ordered the army of Soviet-satellite Bulgaria out of the parts of Macedonia and Thrace it had occupied. This conformed to a Churchill-Stalin agreement, in October 1944, by which Britain was to regain its influence over Greece in return for Russian influence over Bulgaria, Hungary, and Rumania.

By the end of 1944 ELAS controlled all but large cities and other centers occupied by the British army. The Communist guerrillas refused to surrender their arms unless rival guerrilla groups did the same. When no agreement could be reached, civil war broke out all over Greece until the British, using 75,000 troops, put down the rebellion.

After a British-arranged cease-fire in February 1945, ELAS surrendered many of its weapons to the British-supported government which immediately began a wave of repression. As the repressions increased, many of the ELAS leaders, fearing for their lives, fled to the hills and by the end of the year civil war had broken out again. For the next year or so the war grew in violence with the most brutal acts imaginable on both sides. The rebels were now aided by the neighboring Communist countries, Yugoslavia, Bulgaria, and Albania, but the relationship was difficult, because the Greeks realized that Yugoslavia and Bulgaria had their eyes on Greek territory. Supposedly they were all Communists together but—and this has invariably proved the case—they were nationalists first. No significant aid came from Russia.

The struggle continued, and by early 1947 the British had to admit they could no longer handle the situation. If it hadn't been for American intervention, the Communist-led ELAS would probably have won. But Washington, as Richard J. Barnet has stated:

. . . developed a rationale to justify a moral crusade in behalf of an inefficient and reactionary government. The argument . . . went like this: The United States had to make a choice between supporting temporarily a bad democratic government (democratic in form) and allowing an armed minority under Soviet direction to fasten a Communist dictatorship permanently upon Greece. . . .

Crucial to this analysis besides the dubious use of the term "democratic" was the assumption of "Soviet direction." As we have seen the Soviets in fact were giving neither aid nor direction. A few months later they would vainly seek to persuade Yugoslavia to cut off the substantial aid which it was giving. "What do you think," Stalin exclaimed to the Yugoslav vice-premier in early 1948, "that Great Britain and the United States—the United

States, the most powerful state in the world—will permit you to break their line of communication in the Mediterranean? Nonsense. And we have no navy. The uprising in Greece must be stopped, and as quickly as possible." Indeed, the Soviet attitude toward Greece conformed perfectly to the Stalinist pattern. Since the Greek guerrillas had taken action independent of the Red Army and Stalin's direction, the Kremlin viewed them as a nuisance and a possible threat to the diplomatic relations of the Soviet Union. Stalin saw them as potential clients of the Yugoslavs, whose claims to a role of independent political leadership in the Balkans he was already attempting to crush.[5]

In short, despite the American conviction that Greece was the starting point of a Communist campaign of expansion, Stalin not only had nothing to do with the Greek rebellion, he was trying to stop it.

If Stalin was having trouble with the Yugoslavs, Truman was having trouble with Congress. Both the House and the Senate were strongly Republican and, less than two years after the end of the war, not too eager to get involved abroad. A few days after he received the British note, Truman invited bipartisan leaders of both houses to a White House briefing. The new Secretary of State, General Marshall, told the lawmakers of the implications of the British withdrawal from that strategic area. But they did not seem to grasp why the United States should assume costly and dangerous British responsibilities.

Dean Acheson, then Under Secretary of State, didn't like the drift of the conversation and he intervened. He switched the talk from Greece, the rebels, and Great Britain to the threat of Communist Russia. He drew a picture in which the failure to act in Greece would lead to Communist penetration not just in the eastern Mediterranean but in Western Europe as well. Then, in the words of Joseph M. Jones, Acheson went on to "pull out all the stops."

Only two great powers remained in the world, the United States and the Soviet Union. We had arrived at a situation unparalleled since ancient times. Not since Rome and Carthage had there been such a polarization of power on this earth. . . . It was clear that the Soviet Union was aggressive and expanding. For the United States to take steps to strengthen countries threatened with Soviet aggression or Communist subversion was to protect the security of the United States.[6]

This phrase, "Soviet aggression or Communist subversion," is a key to many of America's difficulties in the last twenty years. Outright aggression, the conventional crossing of international frontiers, is easy to establish, but to define "Communist subversion," as the United States has learned in Vietnam, is something else again. If the Communists are citizens of the country involved and are acting in response to a national grievance, are they guilty of "Communist subversion," thus making it justifiable for the United States to intervene? Or are they patriots, revolutionaries, acting according to the principles of the American Declaration of Independence which states that "whenever any Form of Government becomes destructive to these ends, it is the Right of the People to alter or to abolish it, and to institute new Government, laying its foundation on such principles and organizing its powers in such form, as to them shall seem most likely to effect their Safety and Happiness."

It would be facile to say that it is always easy to determine what is subversion and what is legitimate revolution. But the observable fact is that the United States has almost always

since the end of World War II defined *any* Communist movement—even if nationalist, even if there has been no direct
link between that movement and Moscow (or later, Peking)
—as a subversive movement in response to which the United
States feels free to take any action it deems appropriate.

Why is this? In large part because of the terms in which the
Truman Doctrine was explained to Congress and the American people. In Acheson's words, the United States and Russia
"were divided by an unbridgeable ideological chasm," and
he strove to impress this upon the Congress.

Acheson gambled that he could move American politicians not
with the chessboard language of balance of power, the stock in
trade of the professional diplomat and the soldier, but with the
rhetoric of crusade that twice in his lifetime stirred the nation
to do battle on foreign shores.

His instincts were correct. Vandenberg, deeply impressed by
Acheson's presentation, told the President that he must lay these
same facts before the American people if he wanted to get Congressional support for the program. The President must "scare
hell" out of Congress and the people.[7]

Thus the United States came to see the Cold War not as a
struggle between the national interests of two great powers—
and therefore one that could be analyzed coolly—but as a
conflict between two ideologies, between "good," the United
States, and "evil," Communist Russia. And although it has
always been the tendency of nations to clothe differences in
moralistic terms, such a practice seldom causes reason to
triumph over emotion.

To get back to Greece, it seems likely that the possibility
that the guerrillas had fought for reasons of their own and
not as agents of a foreign power was never seriously con-

sidered. Or perhaps that was regarded as irrelevant. The Truman Administration may have been of the conviction— an honest and deeply felt one shared by a large proportion of the American people—that Communism was inherently immoral and that the right of self-determination did not extend that far. This, of course, raises a basic question: Does a nation have the right to choose any government it wants, whether through free elections or through revolution? On how that question is answered depends the judgment of much of American foreign policy since World War II.

The Greek request for American aid was actually first drafted by the United States. Richard Barnet describes how it happened:

On February 23, 1947, Loy Henderson summoned the Greek chargé d'affaires. As the Greek diplomat reported to Athens, the director of the Office of Near Eastern and African Affairs was smiling "as though experiencing some sort of glowing inner satisfaction." Henderson informed the Greek that the United States had decided to take historic measures to aid his country. He then outlined the text of a draft letter of request, and after "protracted discussion" the American and Greek diplomats "prepared in common" a draft, which, the chargé reported, "I was requested to submit urgently, as soon as I got your approval, to the State Department in the name and at the instructions of the Greek government." Henderson stressed that the text "had been drafted with a view to the mentality of Congress. . . . It would also serve to protect the U.S. government against internal and external charges that it was taking the initiative of intervening in a foreign state or that it had been persuaded by the British to take over a bad legacy from them. The note would also serve as a basis for the cultivation of public opinion which was under study." [8]

The note must have been effective. The Senate approved
the legislation requested by Truman on April 22 and the
House on May 9. The United States hoped that "a massive
infusion of American power and money could establish a
stable, moderate, reasonably democratic government and that
the military operations should be regarded as instruments to
set up the preconditions for bringing about political and
social change." [9] This sounds very much like the basis on
which President Kennedy first intervened in Vietnam a
decade and a half later. But the Greek rebels were tough and
the Greek government, as the United States learned to its
dismay, utterly incapable of making progress on basic political and economic problems that were crippling the country.

It took two and a half years to end the rebellion, and
only after massive amounts of American artillery, dive
bombers, and napalm had been sent to Greece. The Greek
government military forces, greatly increased, were placed
under the direct command of more than 250 American Army
"advisers" headed by General James A. Van Fleet. Finally
General Van Fleet authorized a program for "the systematic
removal of whole sections of the population" to separate the
guerrillas from the people who supported them.[10] This, too,
was a tactic later employed in Vietnam. By October 16, 1949
the rebels had taken all the punishment they could and the
guerrilla radio announced a cease-fire.

This victory was judged a great triumph for Harry
Truman. Yet in the spring of 1967, twenty years after U.S.
intervention, Greece, despite continued American aid, still
had not worked out its problems and a right-wing military
junta grabbed power.

Although most of the Congress and the American public

accepted Truman's call to arms and believed that if Communist Russia were not stopped in Greece, it would have to be stopped elsewhere at greater cost, there was, nonetheless, considerable criticism from respectable quarters. Republican Senate leader Robert Taft, an arch conservative, charged Truman with dividing the world into Communist and anti-Communist parts and said he did "not want war with Russia."

And the newspaper columnist, Walter Lippmann, who for decades was perhaps the most astute critic of American foreign policy, wrote concerning the American bypassing of the United Nations: "If the pattern of our conduct in this affair becomes a precedent, we shall have cut a hole in the Charter which will be very difficult to repair." And he remarked prophetically that the United States was "not rich enough to subsidize reaction all over the world or strong enough to maintain it in power." [11]

4

The Marshall Plan
and Containment

Having made the decision to battle Communism wherever
it should appear, the Truman Administration now had
to prepare an overall strategy. For as important as the decision on Greece was, that was only one small area among many
where the forces of the Free World and Communism confronted each other. (The Free World became a favorite
American term for describing in an all-embracing way the
complex system of its allies, supporters, and clients. As anyone
who thought about it realized, however, the Free World
included a great many dictatorships or nondemocratic authoritarian governments in Europe, Asia, and Latin America.
A more precise, but less inspiring, term would have been the
Anti-Communist World, for any nation, whatever its degree
of democracy (or lack of it), was welcome if it were sufficiently
anti-Communist.) Thus evolved in short order the Marshall
Plan and the overall master strategy, the "containment
policy."

The Marshall Plan has often been called, and properly,

40

a classic example of "enlightened self-interest." Shortly after Truman's historic speech of March 12, Secretary of State Marshall, just returned from a trip to Europe, convinced Truman that the continent was desperately in need of help. Not only were people living in misery because of the war-torn economies (and thus worthy of assistance in the old American tradition of helping a neighbor), but a Europe on the verge of economic collapse would be easy prey for the Soviet Union, either by direct action or by the political success of local Communist parties who made up a quarter of the French electorate and a third of the Italian. Furthermore, the American economy needed strong economies in Europe to buy the flood of exports pouring out of American factories more productive than ever before. And American economic intervention could help stop any trend toward socialism and nationalization of industry. So, there was every good reason —both for Europe and the United States—for America to help, and on June 5 at Harvard, Marshall unveiled the plan that was to bear his name and be his greatest monument. He called for economic aid on a scale never before known to man. This was a bold undertaking indeed, for not only was aid of this magnitude unknown, it was being asked of a Congress completely dominated by Republicans who were intent upon spending less money, not more.

That was just one problem. There was a related one even more complex: what to do about the Russians. For more than two years Stalin had been seeking American aid to help reconstruct his devastated land, but the two nations had not been able to agree on terms. Could the United States now offer enormous sums to Western Europe and leave out Eastern Europe? If it did, wouldn't that prove what Stalin had been saying all along, that the United States wanted to divide Europe, control one half of it, while carrying out economic warfare against the other?

There was a further complication. What if the United States offered aid to Russia and its satellites and they accepted? That would raise astronomically the cost to a budget-minded Congress. And more difficult yet, hadn't the Truman Administration just convinced Congress of the necessity to stop the growth of Communism? How could it ask Congress to spend billions to help the Communists?

The State Department was perplexed. It didn't want to help the Russians, it didn't see how Congress would agree to do so, and it feared that Russian and East European participation would put the cost so high that the entire program, East and West, would be rejected. Nonetheless, Truman decided he had no choice but to invite Russia, which immediately after Marshall's Harvard speech had called the plan "a Truman Doctrine with dollars, a useless attempt to save the American economy by dominating the markets of Europe." [1]

Russia accepted the invitation to discuss the plan, immediately moderated its attacks, and sent Foreign Minister V. M. Molotov off on June 26 to the Paris conference with an entourage of eighty-nine economic experts and clerks. This was again a fateful moment in East-West relations, for Russia seemed to be giving the idea serious consideration. But if it was a problem for Washington, it was fully as much a problem for Moscow. Stalin wanted aid very badly but did not want Americans swarming all over Russia administering it. So at the Paris Conference Molotov proposed that each country establish its own recovery program and submit it to Washington.

Britain and France, as the United States wanted them to do, countered with the proposal that Europe as a whole prepare a recovery plan for American consideration. Then, a few days later, June 30, the other Western European nations threw their support to the American plan and Molotov stormed off to Moscow, angrily proclaiming that the Marshall Plan would weaken national sovereignty, revive Germany, lead to American domination of Europe and, most significantly, divide "Europe into two groups of states . . . creating new difficulties in the relations between them." [2]

Since then some Americans have said that Russia's subsequent economic difficulties were its own fault, that it could have had American aid if it had wanted it. But it was not that simple, as political analyst John Spanier explains:

For European cooperation would mean that Russia would have to disclose full information about her economy and allow the United States to have some control in her economic planning, as well as in that of her satellites. This was unthinkable to a totalitarian state; a Communist state could hardly permit capitalists to have a voice in its economic development. Soviet participation would also require the Soviet Union and its satellites to contribute toward Europe's recovery with food and raw materials, in return for help they were receiving from the United States. Thus, the Rusians would actually be helping to stabilize European capitalism. [3]

Again there was a situation where the two systems were simply incompatible. To blame Russia for not accepting the Marshall Plan—and their acceptance would almost certainly have killed it in Congress—is to blame them for refusing to deny their own nature. They had their own economic prejudices just as did the United States, which, after all, would administer the Marshall Plan according to its own standards. Many Americans have thought of the Plan as a disinterested act of generosity. It was generous, to be sure, but there were strictly American purposes as well.

The Marshall Plan was the chief way the American capitalist system made its impact felt in Europe. The ECA (the Economic Cooperation Administration, the U.S. agency that administered the Plan) discouraged European exchange controls, import quotas, tariffs, cartels. American administrators of ECA and American businessmen, who went to Europe in the Marshall Plan years to advise European governments and businessmen, encouraged free and competitive capitalism and the streamlined methods of American business. Frequently they took an even more active part against socialist measures and Socialist parties than against cartels. Many were discouraged that they did not make a more permanent impression and complained of the radicalism of European labor, of the feudal mentality of European businessmen, and of the practice of doing away with one control and then substituting another, for instance, of doing away with an import quota and then getting the same results by a high tariff or an international cartel arrangement.[4]

But whatever the proportion of altruism and self-interest, the Marshall Plan did the job. By pumping $12 billion into the European economy (much of it went right back to the United States in purchases), the Marshall Plan saved the Western European economy and established the foundation for the boom that followed only a few years later. That is not to say, however, that the Plan was entirely successful. It had one very serious shortcoming. Although it saved the

European economy, the benefits did not always filter down to the workingman. To be sure, they were working when otherwise they might not have been, but they could see that the owners and managers were prosperous again while they were still worse off than before the war. Such a situation hardly furthered one of the main American goals of the Plan, luring the workers away from the Communist party. In fact, twenty years after the Marshall Plan the Communist parties were still powerful in Italy and France.

Unprecedented, enormous, and historic as the Marshall Plan was, it was only one element in what became in 1947 the American master plan, the "containment policy," a policy carried out in essentially the same way by every President from Truman to Nixon. This policy was perhaps best described by one of its principal architects, George F. Kennan, who at the time was one of Secretary Marshall's top advisers as head of the State Department's Policy Planning Staff. An article by Kennan, under the pseudonym "X," appeared in the July 1947 issue of *Foreign Affairs*. In this article, which was a sensation, particularly since it almost immediately became known that the author was a senior State Department official, Kennan wrote:

. . . the Kremlin has no compunction about retreating in the face of superior force. And being under the compulsion of no timetable, it does not get panicky under the necessity for such retreat. Its political action is a fluid stream which moves constantly, wherever it is permitted to move, toward a given goal. Its main concern is to make sure that it has filled every nook and cranny available to it in the basin of world power. But if it finds unassailable barriers in its path, it accepts these philosophically and accommodates itself to them. The main thing is that there should always be pressure, unceasing constant pressure, toward the desired goal. There is no trace of any feeling in Soviet psychology that that goal must be reached at any given time. . . .

In these circumstances it is clear that the main element of any United States policy toward the Soviet Union must be that of a long-term, patient but firm and vigilant *containment* [italics mine] of Russian expansive tendencies. It is important to note, however, that such a policy has nothing to do with outward histrionics: with threats or blustering or superfluous gestures of outward "toughness." While the Kremlin is basically flexible in its reaction to political realities, it is by no means unamenable to considerations of prestige. Like almost any other government, it can be placed by tactless and threatening gestures in a position where it cannot afford to yield even though this might be dictated by its sense of realism. . . .

. . . Russia, as opposed to the Western world in general, is still by far the weaker party, . . . Soviet policy is highly flexible, and . . . Soviet society may well contain deficiencies which will eventually weaken its own total potential. This would of itself warrant the United States entering with reasonable confidence upon a policy of firm containment, designed to confront the Russians with unalterable counter-force at every point where they show signs of encroaching upon the interests of a peaceful and stable world. . . .

It would be an exaggeration to say that American behavior unassisted and alone could exercise a power of life and death over the Communist movement and bring about the early fall of Soviet power in Russia. But the United States has it in its power to increase enormously the strains under which Soviet policy must operate, to force upon the Kremlin a far greater degree of moderation and circumspection than it has had to observe in recent years, and in this way to promote tendencies which must eventually find their outlet in either the break-up or the gradual mellowing of Soviet power. For no mystical, Messianic movement—and particularly not that of the Kremlin—can face frustration indefinitely without eventually adjusting itself in one way or another to the logic of that state of affairs.

Kennan has been quoted at length here because it is on this conviction—that the Russians were ever pressing outward and had to be confronted "with unalterable counter-force"—that American foreign policy has been based ever since 1947. But as Kennan pointed out in his memoirs, his views were misunderstood even by the government he was serving in a high capacity. He admits he was wrong for not making it unmistakable in his article that he meant that this counter-force be political not military. Indeed, Kennan not only objects to the military aspects of the containment policy but even to certain aspects of the Truman Doctrine which first signaled it.

Kennan wrote that while approving the United States action in Greece, he took exception to the language of Truman's March 12 message, "primarily because of the sweeping nature of the commitments which it implied." [5] He particularly questioned Truman's statement that "it must be the policy of the United States to support free peoples who are resisting subjugation by armed minorities or by outside pressure." He went on to explain:

This passage, and others as well, placed our aid to Greece in the framework of a universal policy rather than in that of a specific decision addressed to a specific set of circumstances. It implied that what we had decided to do in the case of Greece was something we would be prepared to do in the case of any other country, provided only that it was faced with the threat of "subjugation by armed minorities or by outside pressures."

It seemed to me highly uncertain that we would invariably find it in our interests or within our means to extend assistance to countries that found themselves in this extremity. The mere fact of their being in such a plight was only one of the criteria that had to be taken into account in determining our action. The establishment of the existence of such a threat was only the beginning, not the end, of the process of decision.[6]

And twenty years after the beginning of the containment policy, Kennan wrote that before aiding a nation the United States should also be sure of "the willingness and ability of the threatened people to pick up and bear resolutely the overwhelming portion of the responsibility and effort in their own defense against both direct and indirect aggression—not just to sit back and hedge against the possibility that resistance might not be effective and leave the burden of the struggle to us." [7]

This, of course, has been a key element in much of the criticism of American intervention in Vietnam. While many have questioned the right of the United States to intervene in what they consider a civil war, many others have argued that although the United States was politically justified to intervene, it should not have, on the practical grounds that the South Vietnamese government did *not* have "the willingness and ability . . . to pick up and bear resolutely the overwhelming portion of the responsibility and effort in their own defense. . . ."

Finally, there is one general observation by Kennan that seems particularly pertinent to this discussion of the Cold War:

Throughout the ensuing two decades the conduct of our foreign policy would continue to be bedeviled by people in our own government as well as in other governments who could not free themselves from the belief that all another country had to do, in order to qualify for American aid, was to demonstrate the existence of a Communist threat. Since almost no country was without a Communist minority, this assumption carried very far. As time went on, the firmness of our understanding for these distinctions on the part of our own public and governmental establishment appeared to grow weaker rather than stronger. In the 1960's so absolute would be the value attached, even by people within the government, to the mere existence of a Communist threat, that such a threat would be viewed as calling, in the case of Southeast Asia, for an American response on a tremendous scale, without serious regard even to those main criteria that most of us in 1947 would have thought it natural and essential to apply.[8]

It is on this basis that there has been growing criticism of American foreign policy in recent years. Many people have asked whether the United States—before intervening in, say, Cuba or the Dominican Republic—considers whether the Communist movement (if in truth it is one) is directed by Moscow or Peking or whether it is indigenous, led and peopled by citizens of the country in question, with national goals sought by the very same right of redress used by the rebels in the American Revolution. And before intervening, these critics ask, has the United States demonstrated in what way these revolutions are a threat to American national security?

There were other important events in 1947. In July, Con-

gress established the Department of Defense, integrating the
Army, Navy, and Air Force, each of which had been previ-
ously administered by a separate department. A National
Security Act also established the National Security Council
to advise the President, and the Central Intelligence Agency
(CIA) which brought under one chief a number of intelligence organizations. The first Secretary of Defense was the
previous Secretary of the Navy, James Forrestal, who believed
in a hard line in the Cold War.

Russia was not inactive either. On August 31, rigged elec-
tions in Hungary ended open anti-Communist opposition,
although it never ceased to exist beneath the surface and
would break out again with tragic consequences in 1956.
Three weeks later Russian words followed deed as Andrei
Zhdanov, one of Stalin's lieutenants, proclaimed that the
United States was organizing Western Europe, the Near East,
South America, and China into an anti-Communist bloc.

Stalin's spokesman revived some old Communist rhetoric,
saying that the world was now divided into two camps, a view
Stalin had espoused in his early years in power. In some
respects Zhdanov's announcement paralleled the "two-world"
attitude in the United States. This resemblance seemed
especially strong when Zhdanov, in a warning to the rest
of the socialist camp, declared: "Just as in the past the
Munich policy untied the hands of the Nazi aggressors, so
today concessions to the new course of the United States
and the imperialist camp may encourage its inspirers to be
even more insolent and aggressive." [9]

Change just a few words and it could have been John
Foster Dulles or Dean Rusk speaking. And indeed the
United States had also embarked upon a two-world policy. On

September 2, at U.S. insistence, the Latin American nations at Rio de Janeiro signed the Rio Treaty which formed an alliance in the Western hemisphere clearly designed as a barrier against Communism. This was the beginning of a series of alliances that within a few years completely encircled the earth, alliances that the United States termed defensive and that Russia, naturally, termed offensive. The two great powers simply had entirely different views of the world and it seemed beyond their capacity for them to understand one another.

Perhaps not so incidentally, although the Latin nations had crushing economic problems, the ground rules for the Rio conference were established in such a way that there was no formal discussion of economic aid to Latin America. At this moment the United States was solely concerned with military considerations.

5

Confrontation

IF 1947 was the year in which the Cold War took definite shape, 1948 was the year in which the first direct confrontation occurred. For an anxious while this confrontation raised genuine fears that, only three years after the victorious allies, Russia and the United States, had accepted the surrender of Germany, they themselves would be at war.

Early in the year tensions increased when a Communist coup in Prague put Czechoslovakia firmly in the Russian camp. Poor Czechoslovakia, overrun by Hitler's Germany in 1938, now for the second time in a decade became a satellite of a powerful neighbor. Although the Communist party (38 per cent of the vote) was the largest in Czechoslovakia after the elections of May 1946, President Eduard Beneš and Foreign Minister Jan Masaryk attempted to balance their strategic and vulnerable country between East and West. For a while the West thought they might succeed, particularly when the Czechs expressed an interest in joining the Marshall Plan. But Stalin said No; he feared the results of economic association with the West.

In mid-February, 1948, with the Red Army poised along its frontier, Czechoslovakia began to totter. Premier Klement Gottwald, a Stalinist who was to lead Czechoslovakia for many years, refused Beneš' order to reorganize the police force. Gottwald demanded a new government under his power and a group of Russian leaders flew into Prague and insisted that Beneš capitulate. He did on February 25 and again Czechoslovakia lost its independence, not to recover it for another twenty years—and then only briefly.

Two weeks later Jan Masaryk was found dead beneath his office window in Prague. He was a great patriot, the son of Czechoslovakia's chief founder and first president. The Communists claimed he committed suicide but many in the West, and in Czechoslovakia itself, believed he had been murdered by the Communists. The issue is still not closed and during Czechoslovakia's brief freedom in 1968, the question was reopened.

All history abounds with ironies but none more so than that of the Cold War. Czechoslovakia's desire to join the Marshall Plan no doubt contributed to Stalin's decision to remove the country's last vestiges of independence. But then the Communist coup helped push the Marshall Plan through a reluctant, tight-fisted Congress, for, as Truman observed, the coup "sent a shock throughout the civilized world."

On March 16, Truman made another dramatic appearance before Congress. The Marshall Plan had cleared the Senate 69 to 17 two days earlier, but was still awaiting House action. Speaking somberly, Truman told the two houses of the "increasing threat" to the very "survival of freedom." The Marshall Plan, he said, was not enough; Europe had to have "some measure of protection against internal and external aggression." Again asserting itself was the great American fear of a Russian takeover of Western Europe, a fear which, however unfounded, was nevertheless real. Truman asked for, and eventually got, a new draft law; the old one had been allowed to lapse a year before.

Late in March the House approved the Marshall Plan, and across the Atlantic an event of comparable significance was taking place that same month. On March 17, Britain, France, Belgium, the Netherlands, and Luxembourg signed a 50-year Treaty of Mutual Assistance. The treaty was negotiated with the urgent support of the United States. Truman immediately hailed it, and soon the Administration began working with Senator Vandenberg on a resolution that would tie the United States to the new treaty. The Vandenberg Resolution was passed by the Senate 64 to 4 in June, and immediately the new Under Secretary of State, Robert Lovett, went to Europe for three months of talks to negotiate U.S. entry into the organization that would soon become known as NATO.

Even before these talks were finished, two events which would affect them took place almost simultaneously: the Berlin blockade and the break between Stalin and the Yugoslav Communist leader, Joseph Broz Tito.

Russia had become increasingly worried about Western influence in Germany. It was convinced that a demilitarized, neutral Germany was fundamental to its security but the three western zones of Germany, the most populous and industrialized, were moving steadily toward the West. On

March 6, 1948, after a conference in London, the West announced that the West German economy would be integrated into that of Western Europe and that the three western zones would be combined. This was to be a step toward a "federal form of government" and would bring the great industrial resources of the Ruhr Valley into the Western coalition. The conference also announced a currency reform for the western zones. Russia's response on April 1 was to temporarily restrict the movement of Western military supplies into Berlin.

On June 4 the West told the West Germans they could begin the constitutional processes toward the establishment of the Federal Republic of Germany and two weeks later began issuing the new currency in the three western zones. The Russians protested that the currency—intended to end inflation and black markets—would drive all the valueless old reichsmarks into their zone, so the Russians also introduced a new currency. Then Stalin, unwilling to allow Germany to join the West uncontested, and also facing serious difficulties within his own camp, decided to take a drastic step—perhaps even a reckless one.

On Thursday, June 24, Russia imposed a complete blockade on West Berlin. No formal announcement was made, just a couple of items in a Soviet-controlled newspaper announcing that electricity to the western sectors was limited because of "a technical difficulty." The movement of passengers and freight on the Berlin-Helmstedt railroad line was also blamed on "technical difficulties." [1] The Russians announced, too, that food coming into Berlin from surrounding East Germany would be distributed only in the Soviet sector. The goal presumably was to force the West out of Berlin, or perhaps to force an agreement on all Germany more acceptable to Stalin. In any case it was a bold move to keep West Germany out of the Western alliance.

The West immediately declared it would not be forced out of Berlin, and the American commander in Germany, General Lucius Clay, said that only by war could the Russians get the Americans to leave. While Washington, London, and Paris began urgent talks, Western authorities in their three sectors began to husband food. In an attempt to quiet German fears, they announced that there was enough food on hand for thirty days and plenty of powdered milk for infants and children to replace that which normally came in from East Germany. Despite these measures, the people of West Berlin were still fearful that the West would not be able to supply their sectors, and that the troops would have to pull out, surrendering the enclave deep in the Soviet zone of Germany.

The next day, Friday, the Soviet commander, Marshal Sokolovsky, accused the West of refusing reasonable Russian proposals in the Allied Control Council, of attempting to ruin the economic life of Berlin by bringing illegal Western marks into Berlin, and of attempting to divide Germany. All this without any direct reference to the blockade.

The story was, of course, headline news the world over and there were many in the Western world ready to pull out of Berlin. This was only three years after the war and many people in the West simply could not see the point of going to the brink of another war on behalf of a nation that had in the immediate past brought destruction to all of Europe and caused millions of deaths and misery beyond reckoning.

While the Western capitals were trying to make up their minds, General Clay acted. He was convinced that it would be politically disastrous for the West to pull out of Berlin. He immediately thought of trying to supply Berlin by air, an idea that occurred to a number of people at the same time. The British, indeed, had airlifted in six and one half tons of supplies for their garrison on June 25 and were considering an airlift for the civilian population. Clay talked to General Curtis LeMay, the American air commander in Germany, and got him to mobilize all possible aircraft. Meanwhile, Clay told Washington, which still couldn't make up its mind, that he didn't expect armed conflict, that the main problem was the morale of the West Berliners. But that turned out not to be a problem; despite intensive Soviet propaganda, the Berliners rallied behind their leaders. However, the logistic problem was immense. Berlin needed 2,000 tons of supplies a day and it seemed that American aircraft would be lucky to reach a third of that total.

As General LeMay tried to scrape up additional planes, Truman ordered that every U.S. plane in Europe be pressed into service. At that time he, and everyone else, was not thinking about supplying Berlin indefinitely by air but of augmenting supplies to gain time for a diplomatic solution. There seemed to be three possible decisions for the West: to pull out of Berlin at some appropriate time so as to avoid the chance of war over the divided city or at least eliminate U.S. vulnerability to repeated crises; to defend the Western position at all costs; to stay on in Berlin for the time being but to postpone any ultimate decision.

On Monday Harry Truman made his decision. Although his top advisers did not all agree, Truman said with charac-

teristic decisiveness that the United States was going to stay
and that there was to be no more discussion on that point.
Evidently he was persuaded by the argument that withdrawal
would cause all Europe to lose faith in American commitments and encourage the spread of Communism. No one,
of course, knows whether that would have happened, but
the need to honor American commitments has been advanced
at virtually every crisis in the Cold War since then; it was
particularly invoked by Dean Rusk more than fifteen years
later whenever it was suggested that the United States withdraw from its disastrous entanglement in Vietnam.

By the next day, Tuesday, June 29, it began to look as
if the airlift could be more than a temporary expedient.
Britain sent a hundred Royal Air Force planes and the
United States added planes from Alaska and the Caribbean
to those already in Europe. Yet the three democratic parties
in Berlin remained dubious that an airlift could succeed and
pushed their appeal to the United Nations, an appeal that
eventually foundered on a Soviet veto.

On July 6 the United States, Britain, and France gave
similar notes to the Russian ambassadors protesting the
blockade as "a clear violation of existing agreements concerning the administration of Berlin by the four occupying
powers." [2] They also said they would be prepared to negotiate but only after the blockade had been lifted. The next
day American Skymasters began flying coal into Berlin.
Although it was pretty clear now that the West could fly
in enough food, there was grave concern about the winter.
Vast amounts of coal would be needed for heat and electricity, and there was considerable doubt that enough could
be stockpiled even if the Allies began months in advance.

By July 10 General Clay became convinced by Russia's caution that it did not want to risk war. He suggested that the United States break the blockade by sending an armed convoy across East Germany to West Berlin. Washington turned this down, wisely deciding that this might be too much of a challenge to the Russians.

On July 14 the Russians turned down the Western protest notes, saying it, too, was prepared to negotiate but that it would not limit the talks to Berlin alone, since that question had to be considered as part of the question of Germany as a whole. It also said it would not lift the blockade. The Russians went on to declare that "Berlin lies in the center of the Soviet zone and is a part of that zone," and that out of concern for the population of Berlin they would, if necessary, supply the entire city. It is doubtful that the West Berliners were moved by that expression of concern.

By autumn it became apparent that the Western airlift was succeeding and that even the bitter cold winter would not bring the determined West Berliners to their knees. In early 1949 Russia began to hint that there could be a way out of the impasse. But until negotiations finally began, the Russians imposed the blockade more tightly than ever, and it was not uncommon for anti-Communist West Berliners to be kidnapped and disappear into the Russian zone as the spy organizations of both sides carried on a shadowy war.

In March informal talks at the UN between American Ambassador Philip Jessup and Russian Ambassador Jacov Malik began to progress. Toward the end of the month Malik told Jessup that if a definite date were set for a foreign ministers' meeting, Russia would end the blockade. A date

was set and on May 5, Washington, London, Paris, and
Moscow announced that the Russian blockade and the allied
counterblockade would be lifted on May 12 and that the
Big Four foreign ministers would meet on May 23.

The Russian blockade of 324 days had failed. The West
had scored an enormous propaganda victory and much more
than that, for supplying West Berlin entirely by air was an
almost incredible feat. Because of the blockade, West Germany had moved closer to the West than ever before (and
farther away from Russia), American airpower in Europe
had grown tremendously, and Berlin had been established
as such a symbol that it would be impossible for decades to
come for the United States to abandon it. Perhaps if the
Russians had nibbled away at West Berlin, as they began to
do years later, they would have been more successful. But
history does not allow replays and it is clear that Stalin
made a monumental blunder, one that added greatly to
the growing intensity of the Cold War.

Yet for all the attention Stalin must have devoted to the
Berlin blockade, he could have been no less concerned about
a development within the Communist camp. From the earliest days of the Bolshevik revolution in 1917, Moscow had
been the undisputed Rome of Communism. All Communist
roads led to Moscow, and back and forth along them traveled
the leaders of Communist parties the world over. Lenin's
word, and then Stalin's, was law in virtually every Communist party in the world. Whatever Moscow ordered was done,
particularly in the Communist parties in Europe and America.

But eventually Stalin came to realize—or perhaps it was
an unconscious realization—that ideological interests and

national interests did not always coincide and he, like all national leaders, put national considerations first. Thus, the Communist parties elsewhere often had to follow policies that twisted and turned and contradicted earlier policies. Usually Stalin gave orders that served Russian national interests, and if any foreign Communists questioned them—which few did—they were ordered to do as they were told.

Stalin developed an impatience for any Communist movement that was not totally, unquestioningly loyal to Moscow. If he had to sacrifice the interests of another Communist party to the interests of Moscow, he didn't hesitate for a second, as was the case when he abandoned the Communists in Greece, and when he ordered the parties in Italy and France to take vigorous action against the Marshall Plan at the cost of their own political strength and of their national interest.

It's hard to see exactly what Yugoslavia's leader, Tito, was guilty of in Stalin's eyes. He was certainly a loyal Communist and he never questioned Stalin's pre-eminence as the leader of Communists everywhere. But in Stalin's last years the Soviet leader, always suspicious, became almost paranoiacally so. Whenever Tito showed the slightest reluctance to follow Moscow's orders on all matters, Stalin became enraged, reportedly declaring: "I will shake my little finger—and there will be no more Tito."

But the crafty Stalin for once did not take into account all the facts. Tito was not like the other leaders in satellite nations. He did not owe his job to Stalin. A great guerrilla fighter, he had liberated Yugoslavia from the Germans without the Red Army. He was a national hero who had mass support, unlike other Communist leaders who relied on

minority elites and the Red Army. Also Yugoslavia did not
have a common frontier with Russia and since it had a long
coastline, it could not be isolated. Perhaps most important,
Tito was a brave man. He did not tremble before Stalin's
threats, and his secret police were more than a match for
Stalin's when the Russian tried to overthrow him by a coup.

Even Stalin's rage, however, could not entirely overcome
his native caution. No doubt Russia could have conquered
Yugoslavia by sheer force but Stalin must have been convinced that Tito would fight. An open battle against a determined opponent of unquestioned skill and courage would
have been foolhardy and Stalin was no fool. Instead, he called
a special meeting of the Cominform (Communist Information Bureau, the formal organization of Communist nations)
in Bucharest, and on June 28, 1948, Tito and Yugoslavia
were expelled from the Soviet camp.

This was another incredible blunder. In the first place,
Yugoslavia had wanted to stay within the Communist group
and any differences between the two nations could have been
worked out, as indeed they were when Khrushchev came to
power. But Yugoslavia's expulsion caused it, of necessity, to
put lines out to the West. Most important, it demonstrated
to the Communist world—although the United States at first
did not understand its significance—that to Russia Communism and nationalism were incompatible in any other nation but Russia itself. Stalin immediately embarked upon a
bloody purge within the satellite nations to rip out any in-
cipient Titos.

What Russia understood all too well, but what, tragically,
the American government did not, was that the age of
monolithic Communism was over. Both Russians and Amer-

icans had viewed the world as divided unequivocally into two camps. And the Americans particularly believed that Communism, as directed by Moscow, was one single mighty force that had to be opposed everywhere at all times, at any cost. But Russia had learned the hard way that its days of absolute dominance were over. It now knew what it had always feared, that nationalism was a greater force than Communism and that any Communist party that Moscow could not control might well set off on its own course, a course that might not be in Russia's national interest.

This, no doubt, explained Stalin's ambivalent attitude toward the Chinese Communists. On the one hand, he wanted to help them because they were fellow Communists. On the other, he realized that once Mao was in power, national interests would predominate and that the inevitable national rivalry between two giant neighbors would weaken Moscow's sway over Peking. Thus, it was in his interest to help the Communists but not so much that they would overthrow Chiang Kai-shek, for as long as the Chinese Communists were dependent on Moscow, they would be subservient.

If the West, particularly the United States, had recognized that the monolithic period of Communism ended in 1948, the Cold War might never have developed to the tragic dimensions it did, with the Korean and Vietnam Wars and their enormous cost in lives, misery, and divisiveness.

6

The Closing of the Ring

EARLY in 1949, after proposing mutual withdrawal, Russia withdrew its troops from North Korea where they had been sent to accept the surrender of the Japanese armies. Within six months the United States would pull its troops out of South Korea, leaving that ancient but now divided land to be contested by the two authoritarian leaders, the Communist Kim Il Sung in the North and the right-wing Syngman Rhee in the South.

At the time, however, that did not seem important. The Truman Administration had but one goal in the spring of 1949: getting Congressional authority to join the North Atlantic Treaty Organization (NATO), a military alliance thought to be a necessary shield against Russian expansion into Western Europe. The treaty was signed April 4 by the United States and Belgium, Canada, Denmark, France, Great Britain, Iceland, Italy, Luxembourg, the Netherlands, Norway, and Portugal, and was extended two years later to Greece and Turkey.

64

The treaty then went before the U.S. Senate for ratification. The hearings were most informative, particularly in view of later American policy. Dean Acheson told Senator Henry Cabot Lodge (later to be defeated by the young John F. Kennedy for the Senate seat, then to become Ambassador to the UN, Richard Nixon's running mate in 1960, twice Ambassador to Saigon and, in 1969, chief U.S. negotiator at the Vietnam peace talks in Paris) that no one "at the present time" planned to follow NATO with "a Mediterranean pact, and then a Pacific pact, and so forth." [1] But this, of course, is exactly what did happen when John Foster Dulles became Secretary of State under Dwight Eisenhower. Thus, the NATO pact was the first and most important link in the chain of alliances that would before long entirely enclose the Communist world.

The Senate agreed with Acheson that the UN could not be trusted to defend Europe and there was also agreement that NATO was "to create not merely a balance of power, but a preponderance of power," so the United States could negotiate with Russia from "a position of strength." This conviction that the United States must always be much stronger than Russia has been an article of faith with every President and Secretary of State since then, up to and including President Nixon and Secretary William Rogers. Never have any of these American statesmen given credence to the argument that a position of American superiority forces the Russians to try to catch up, forcing the Americans to try to widen the gap again, and the Russians to try harder to catch up, and so on, until there is a never-ending escalation of the arms race. Such an indefinite spiraling means no more security for either nation at any stage than there was at the beginning, despite the expenditure of staggering sums of money that could have been used by both nations for more productive purposes. Since each side already possesses enough nuclear weaponry to destroy the other, additional armaments add nothing further to the deterrent.

The Senate also attempted to find out exactly what the military significance of NATO was, since its armies alone would never be enough to withstand the massive Red Army if ever it should strike into Western Europe. The chief defense of Western Europe—then as now—was the belief that any Russian strike would mean an atomic response from the United States, and therefore a war that Russia could not hope to win. In any case, Acheson told the Senators, when asked if the Administration planned to send "substantial" numbers of U.S. men to strengthen Europe's defenses: "The answer to that question, Senator, is a clear and absolute No." And when asked if Truman planned to rearm Germany, Acheson replied, "We are very clear that the disarmament and demilitarization of Germany must be complete and absolute." But within a year or so the Truman Administration was to make a complete turnabout on both issues, largely in response to the war which had by that time begun in Korea. Perhaps the most succinct summary of the significance of NATO was made by the powerful Texas Democrat, Senator Tom Connally: "The Atlantic Pact is but the logical extension of the Monroe Doctrine."

Although the Senate asked some tough questions, it soon ratified the NATO Treaty and Truman signed it on July 23, 1949. But the NATO alliance did not escape criticism. Many non-Communist leftist groups in Western Europe, particularly the more liberal wing of the British Labor Party, argued that the emphasis on the military was the result of a superficial analysis of the world situation. They maintained that there was no immediate danger of a military strike by Russia, that it was still too weakened by the war ended just four years before to start another.

These critics also said that the people of Europe, East and West, were primarily concerned with recovering from the war and that the United States, by making arms the first priority, was actually increasing tensions and diverting the West from the basic political and economic reforms that alone could defeat Communism. The best way to stop the spread of Communism, they insisted, was to give vast amounts of economic aid to the underdeveloped nations.

Some of those concerned about possible Soviet aggression wondered if NATO wouldn't cause an irrevocable split between East and West, and even if it might not invite the very attack it was meant to prevent. Also, supporters of the UN asked if a military alliance outside the organization didn't violate the spirit of the Charter.

However valid these concerns, the Truman Administration was convinced that American security depended on NATO, and it has been a keystone of American policy ever since. Nonetheless, there is no doubt that NATO alarmed Russia. It regarded the formation of NATO as a hostile act. Yet, just as there was no real reason for the West to expect a Russian attack—all considerations of intent aside, Russia was simply too weak—there was no real reason for Russia to expect a thrust from NATO. It also was too weak and indeed has never reached the goals set for it by the Pentagon.

Again, as has so often been the case during the Cold War, each side reacted according to its fears rather than in response to actual danger.

Meanwhile, in the East, Mao Tse-tung's Communists had gradually overcome the Nationalists, despite the numerical superiority of Chiang Kai-shek's Nationalist armies and despite the American aid in money and matériel to Chiang. The Communists had superior strategy (Mao has long been recognized as one of history's great guerrilla warriors) and superior dedication, whereas Chiang's leadership was often corrupt and incompetent. By mid-November 1948 the head of the American Advisory Group in China said the Nationalists had "the world's worst leadership." And by February 1949 about half of the Nationalist troops were lost, most by defection, and more than three quarters of the American matériel given Chiang had been captured by the Communists. By April Chiang's government was staggering and his supporters in and outside the American Congress, the so-called China Lobby, were outraged. They demanded that President Truman do something to save China. There was, however, absolutely nothing Truman could do short of committing huge American armies to the struggle, and no one, not even the most militant Chiang supporters, was willing to do that.

By August 1949 the American Administration knew the game was up for Chiang and on the 5th, Dean Acheson released the now-famous China "White Paper," 1054 pages designed to prove the Administration's case that "the unfortunate but inescapable fact is that the ominous result of the civil war in China was beyond the control of the government of the United States. . . . It was the product of internal Chinese forces, forces which this country tried to influence but could not."

In the introduction to the paper Acheson made another statement that opponents of the Vietnam War have often recalled. He said that the only alternative would have been a "full-scale intervention" of American men that "would have been resented by the mass of the Chinese people, would have diametrically reversed our historic policy, and would have been condemned by the American people."

Acheson was convinced that hostility between China and Russia was bound to emerge, that Chinese nationalism would resist Russian overlordship, that Mao might become another Tito. There was even the hope in some Washington quarters that Mao might move toward the United States, for, remember, at the time the United States considered Russia the main enemy.

According to Acheson's analysis, the United States would first have to disentangle itself from Chiang Kai-shek.

Until this disassociation had been completed [Acheson believed], the United States would remain identified with the government rejected by the Chinese people. This could only foster the growth of anti-American sentiment in China. It was precisely this which had to be avoided, for the attention of the Chinese people should not be diverted from the Soviet Union's detachment of the northern provinces. Russia's actions would unmask her real purposes. Under no circumstance, Acheson emphasized, must we "seize the unenviable position which the Russians have carved out for themselves. We must not undertake to deflect from the Russians to ourselves the righteous anger, and the wrath, and the hatred of the Chinese people which must develop." Only by disengaging ourselves from Chiang Kai-shek could the United States exploit the alleged clash of interests between China and Russia.[2]

Many people have since wondered what would have happened if the United States had followed that policy—could the Korean War and the long hostility which followed have been avoided? The answer must remain mere speculation, for the United States soon adopted a position just the opposite of that proposed by Acheson.

Several things influenced Washington's decision. First, the China Lobby rained abuse on the Truman Administration, accusing it of "losing China just as it had Poland." The fact that neither China nor Poland was America's to lose seemed irrelevant. Because the criticism was so sustained, and seemed to be spreading beyond the China Lobby, Truman moved cautiously. When the People's Republic of China proclaimed itself at the end of September, Acheson announced that the United States would not recognize the Communist government.

Then, in late September, Harry Truman announced that the Russians had successfully tested an atomic bomb. Thus, years before U.S. military planners (except for a few scientists) thought Russia would get the bomb, American atomic monopoly was ended. Never again, even though its military superiority has persisted to this day, would the United States stand in such a position of unique and unchallengeable strength.

Both the Communist conquest of China and the Russian bomb had a profound effect, not only on the government but on the American people. The threat of Communist aggression loomed large and it was then, in the final months of 1949, that one of the most shameful periods in American history began—a period that has taken its name, McCarthyism, from that of its most notorious figure, Republican Senator Joseph McCarthy of Wisconsin.

During the next few years many Americans were bewildered and frightened. They were told by right-wing extremists that Truman and Acheson had "lost" China (and later North Korea) because they had not been tough enough on the Communists. They heard that Russia would not have gotten the bomb if it had not been for treasonous acts by certain Americans. Fear fed on fear, fear that was compounded by frustration during the two long years of stalemate in the unpopular Korean War. And in the last years of the Truman Administration, such Senators as McCarthy, Homer Capehart, Richard Nixon, and others charged that Communists had influence in high places.

The Administration itself, panicked because these charges were widely believed, instituted a series of loyalty checks unprecedented in American history. Unorthodoxy became equated with disloyalty and it is no exaggeration to say that the American society was consumed by suspicion. Despite the almost total lack of evidence of any significant Communist influence in government or elsewhere—for the suspicion spread to schools and colleges, motion pictures, broadcasting and publishing, indeed to every aspect of American life—the accusations grew more extreme as the years went on. Senator McCarthy's reckless charges—not a single one of which was ever proved—terrorized the nation so that even many brave men were afraid to stand up to him. Men lost their jobs, had their reputations ruined.

Ironically, the most savagely attacked for being "soft on Communism" were Harry Truman and Dean Acheson, the

very two men who more than any others had convinced
America of the dangers of Communism. They became victims
of the fears they first raised, although they had meant great
danger from Communism abroad—not at home. However,
this was not a time for such distinctions.

It would be impossible for anyone who had not lived
through it to comprehend the hysteria, the hate, and the fear
which in those years convulsed America. Finally McCarthyism exhausted itself, consumed perhaps by its own excesses.
This was the first, but not the last, torment self-imposed on
America because of the Cold War.

And while the first shudders of McCarthyism began to
spread across the land, the Army made its own move. Convinced of the inevitability of a clash between Russia and the
United States, it decided that West Germany, deadly enemy
just four years before, must be rearmed and it persisted in
this even though Truman and Acheson at first rejected the
proposal. They knew that such a course would horrify America's chief allies, Britain and France, indeed would anger
many Americans. They knew, too, that it would cause tremors
of alarm in Russia and in all the Iron Curtain countries
which had been ravaged by Hitler.

7

From Confrontation
to War

1950 BEGAN with a speech by Dean Acheson which became
much more famous months after he delivered it than it was
at the time. On January 12 Acheson, with acute perception,
declared that nationalism not Communism had become the
most significant movement in the world, and he suggested
that the United States and not Russia might become China's
best friend because of Russia's attempt to dominate her vast,
populous, but weak neighbor.

Acheson defined America's "defensive perimeter" as running from the Aleutian Islands off Alaska to Japan, the
Ryukyu Islands, down to the Philippines. He did not include
Korea within this perimeter (which had been defined in the
same terms the year before by General Douglas MacArthur),
and critics later pointed to Acheson's speech as an invitation
to North Korea to invade the South. However, Acheson did
say that the United States had special economic responsibilities in Japan—and Korea.

He also suggested that "subversion and penetration" and

not outright aggression were the main threats to peace in Asia. Subversion and penetration were indeed threats but he was quite wrong about outright aggression. However, no one else expected the invasion either, and the speech seemed at the time simply a wide-ranging one that did not restrict the United States to any particular course of action.

In these deceptively quiet months a secret document was being shaped in the National Security Council which would formalize the direction American foreign policy had been taking since at least early 1947. NSC-68 recommended to President Truman, and he accepted the recommendation, that the United States no longer attempt to "distinguish between national and global security." This meant, in short, that any Communist advance anywhere in the world was seen as a threat to American security, a conviction that has served as the basis for the foreign policy of every President since. It allows of no distinctions and commits the United States to respond promptly and regardless of the cost all over the world.

This conviction, of course, is open to challenge, for it seems evident that while the assumption of power by Communists in one part of the world might well threaten the United States, such assumption elsewhere might not. Nor does this policy make any distinction between those local Communists whose primary loyalties are national and those whose first loyalty is to Moscow or Peking. This is a crucial distinction, for if there is one thing certain in the second half of the twentieth century, it is that nationalism, wherever powerful neighbors will allow it, has always triumphed over all other considerations. Thus, many critics have argued, America's almost reflex response to the word "Communism" has misled it into policies in Guatemala, Lebanon, Cuba, the Dominican Republic, and, most tragically, Vietnam that have actually not been in America's best interests.

In May of 1950, the last peaceful month the United States was to know for three long years, an interesting footnote to history took place. George Kennan, one of the chief architects of the policy of containment, retired from the State Department after a dispute with Secretary Acheson. Kennan had come to dislike the direction of American policy. He believed that the Marshall Plan was a valid act in the Soviet-American competition, but he was concerned about NATO; he thought it put too much emphasis on the military and could cause a permanent split between East and West.

But all these musings must have seemed trivial at 9:26 P.M. on June 24 when Washington received the shocking news that North Korean forces had poured across the 38th parallel in an all-out invasion of South Korea.

There is still no clear understanding why Kim Il Sung's forces chose that time to strike across the arbitrary line dividing the two halves of Korea. The conventional view is that Russia ordered Kim to attack or at least permitted him to. That may be true, but if so, one might well wonder why the Russian Ambassador at the UN, Jacov Malik, continued to absent himself from the Security Council which he was boycotting for excluding the People's Republic of China in favor of Nationalist China. Perhaps it was just an oversight, or perhaps Russia did not think the Security Council would take any significant action. Or perhaps it was just a classic bureaucratic case of the left hand not knowing what the right was doing.

Whatever the reason—and it does seem unlikely that Kim,

who was close to Moscow, would have acted without Russia's consent—the North Koreans did march, thus ending the war of words that Kim and the autocratic old Syngman Rhee had been hurling at each other across the parallel. Actually, it had often been more than words, for on September 2, 1949, the UN Commission for Korea had warned of a possible civil war because of the sporadic and sometimes heavy fighting already breaking out along the parallel.

Following Russian tanks shipped just two months before, North Korean troops hit hard while Pyongyang Radio proclaimed—as invaders usually do—that the other side had struck first. When the State Department received the news that Saturday night, Truman was at home in Independence, Missouri. Acheson informed him straightaway and the President returned immediately to the White House. Although Washington had to consider the possibility that the Korean invasion was the opening move in a coordinated Sino-Soviet campaign, Truman at first acted cautiously. He ordered General MacArthur, the commander in Tokyo, to send supplies to the South Korean troops.

Within a couple of days, however, Truman took an action which, although presumably done for military reasons, took on political significance. He ordered the Seventh Fleet into the China Sea between the mainland and Formosa where Chiang had fled with the remnants of his defeated armies. Until then both Washington and Peking had assumed it was only a matter of months before Mao completed the successful revolution by capturing Formosa. Truman, who had intended a hands-off policy, thus intervened directly in the Chinese civil war and antagonized the new government.[1]

Almost immediately, the UN Security Council—dominated by the United States—passed an American resolution terming North Korea an aggressor, calling for a cessation of hostilities, and asking for a withdrawal behind the 38th parallel. The vote was 9 to 0 with Yugoslavia abstaining and Russia, as noted earlier, absent. But when the North Koreans continued to rush down the peninsula, Truman decided, reluctantly, that the United States must take a direct hand. Although it was a unilateral decision, Washington wanted UN blessings, so the Security Council in another urgent meeting passed a resolution recommending that UN members "furnish such assistance to the Republic of Korea as may be necessary to repel the armed attack and to restore international peace and security in the area." Britain, France, Nationalist China, Cuba, Ecuador, and Norway joined the United States in voting for the resolution. Yugoslavia voted against; Egypt and India abstained; and Russia was still absent—a blunder, for it could have vetoed the resolution and made it more difficult, although not impossible, for the United States to get UN authorization.

As the situation in Korea worsened, Truman on Thursday, less than a week after the invasion, authorized the use of the first American ground troops. But he was uneasy. "I wanted to take every step necessary to push the North Koreans back behind the 38th parallel. But I wanted to make sure that we would not become so deeply committed in Korea that we could not take care of other situations as might develop." [2] This is an absolutely crucial point. The United States goal was specific and limited: to restore the situation as it existed at the time of the invasion, to reestablish the frontier at the 38th parallel, not invade North Korea.

MacArthur told Truman he had not gone far enough, and

the next day the President authorized him to use all forces at his command and to blockade the entire Korean coastline. The United States was now fully committed, and so too was the United Nations—with the result that to this day the United States refers to the American troops in Korea as UN forces. But the fact is that the United States had made a unilateral decision to intervene, and that virtually all the UN forces other than the South Korean were American (although there were token contingents from other nations that fought, often heroically). The commands came directly from U.S. headquarters in Tokyo and Washington, with the UN having absolutely no say in command decisions. It was an American operation under the UN flag. This is not to say that the American decision to intervene was not justified; most would agree that it was.

Although the actual fighting was going on in Korea, the main American foreign policy emphasis still lay on the security of Europe. The defense of South Korea, Washington said, would reassure NATO that the United States would defend its commitments at all costs. And Washington made it clear that it would not divert so many resources to Asia that it was weakened in Europe. This, as we have noted before, has been a hallmark of American policy: to meet all challenges so that our enemies will be discouraged and our allies encouraged that we will meet our commitments to them. But the question long has been: did we really have as many commitments as we said we had, and were all these commitments vital to American security?

For the first two months of the Korean conflict, despite heavy American reinforcements, despite the blockade, despite the heavy pounding by American airpower, the U.S. and

South Korean armies were in full retreat. For weeks it looked as if it were just a matter of time before the North Koreans pushed the allies into the sea. But by the end of August the North Koreans, their longer supply lines vulnerable to American airpower, began to stall. Now the allies had numerical superiority. What had seemed a hopeless rout had been saved, mainly due to overwhelming air support. The North Koreans paused, gathered their strength, and then plunged violently forward in what they hoped would be the final assault. The allies' forces gave, but then, when it no longer seemed possible, held.

The tide turned when MacArthur made a bold—some military men have argued reckless—amphibious landing behind North Korean lines at Inchon. Reckless or not, it succeeded and the Americans for the first time took the offensive. After a fierce battle in which the North Koreans put up heroic resistance and suffered awesome casualties, the Americans retook Seoul, the South Korean capital.

As the Americans and South Koreans fought their way north, Washington had to make another policy decision. Although the goal of American intervention had been to restore the original frontier, now, with military successes, Washington began to consider taking all of North Korea. Congressional elections were approaching, the China Lobby was shouting that not to go north would be appeasement, and the chance did seem to be at hand both to unify Korea and destroy a Communist government. Also, Americans have always wanted clear-cut decisions; they have seldom been able to understand that in a complex world unconditional victories can cost more than they are worth.

Whatever the reason, Truman decided to strike north. But

he was still concerned about Soviet or Chinese entry into the war if the United States crossed the 38th parallel. Thus, he gave MacArthur, who was eager to go all the way to the Chinese border, curious orders:

MacArthur was to conduct the necessary military operations either to force the North Koreans behind the 38th parallel or to destroy their forces. If there was no indication of threat of entry of Soviet or Chinese Communist elements in force . . . [he] was to extend his operations north of the parallel and to make plans for the occupation of North Korea . . . no ground operations should take place north of the 38th parallel in the event of Soviet or Chinese Communist entry.

As military experts have pointed out, these orders did not make sense. Only after MacArthur had fully committed himself would the intervention take place that was the condition on which the commitment should not be made.[3]

If MacArthur noticed the contradiction in these orders, it may have seemed academic, for he was convinced that China would not be able to intervene, that it would not dare to, and that if it did, there would be, as he told Truman at a meeting on Wake Island on October 15, "the greatest slaughter." The Chinese, though, went to great efforts to convince the United States that China would indeed intervene if Americans crossed the 38th parallel. In specific language to Indian Ambassador Panikkar in Peking, meant to be passed on to Washington, Premier Chou En-lai said the Chinese did not care if South Korean forces went north but that if American troops did, China would enter the war.

Since Truman had made it abundantly clear that he did not want American troops to fight Chinese, it can only be surmised that Washington thought China was bluffing, that it would not intervene or that it would not be able to do so in significant degree. Whatever the reason, the United States got the UN General Assembly (the Russians and their veto had returned to the Security Council) to adopt a resolution authorizing, in effect, the military reunification of Korea.

Of these decisions in Washington and at the UN, Max Freedman of the *Manchester* (England) *Guardian* wrote in April, 1961: "It is clear now, though all was in doubt at the time, that the United States blundered into one of the supreme mistakes of its history when it discounted Mr. Panikkar's warning about Chinese intervention in North Korea."

Not only did the American move lead to Sino-American military conflict, poisoning relations between them for decades to come, but it had immeasurable influence on the United Nations. Many Americans have thought that the Korean conflict was the UN's finest hour, but there are others who dispute that. A good case can be made for the American intervention and for UN support of it. It is around the decision of October 7 when the UN General Assembly authorized the United States to conquer North Korea that questions arise. There is no doubt about the vote. It was clearly in support of the United States: 45 in favor, with 5 Communist votes against and 7 abstentions (Egypt, Lebanon, Syria, Yemen, Saudi Arabia, Yugoslavia, and India). But it can be argued that the UN should not take sides in a Cold War dispute but should instead attempt to mediate it. Acting to restore the previous situation was one thing; acting to change the previous situation in favor of the United States was another.

Russia and, particularly, China have always declared that

this action by the UN was illegal and it has continued to be China's basic criticism of the UN. In any case, whether "legal" or not, such a decision could not have been taken a decade or so later when new Asian and African nations began swelling the UN's membership. For then, even though the United States as the world's most powerful nation still dominated the UN, the new members of the General Assembly were not so eager to commit it to either side in the Cold War. And in the Security Council the Russians, who now never absented themselves, still had the veto.

But for better or for worse, the American troops marched north, with MacArthur, to the dismay of the Defense Department, ignoring what few restraints it still imposed upon him. He ordered the Air Force to bomb the bridges crossing the Yalu River from China; Washington countermanded the order. He was going too far. Still the allied troops pushed forward, and in early November they encountered the first Chinese "volunteers" who hit and then faded away. Possibly they wanted to see what the Washington response would be to their presence. Perhaps they thought Washington would realize that they weren't bluffing and would pull back to avoid a direct clash with the Chinese.

Washington didn't know what to do. It didn't want to fight the Chinese, but because of the increased Republican membership in Congress, it didn't want to halt the advance either. And neither MacArthur nor Washington knew how many Chinese had crossed the Yalu. Perhaps fifty or sixty thousand, they thought.

MacArthur pushed ahead. On November 23, the U.S. troops celebrated Thanksgiving, and the next day Mac-Arthur, supremely confident, issued a victory communiqué as he opened what he thought was to be the final offensive. At first there seemed to be no opposition and in one sector the Americans actually reached the Yalu. Then suddenly the Chinese materialized, hit hard at the advancing allies and soon had smashed a breach in their line. Within a couple of days MacArthur's final attack had turned to retreat and then to flight. The Chinese army, scorned by MacArthur, had defeated the much better-equipped Americans. China had proved at least two points: that it was a military force to be reckoned with and that the Americans were not irresistible. As the military writer, General S. L. A. Marshall said in his *The River and the Gauntlet,* the Chinese army was "a phantom which cast no shadow. Its every secret—its strength, its position, and its intention—had been kept to perfection, and thereby it was doubly armed. . . ."

There was consternation in Washington. Truman and his top advisers decided against war with China. They were afraid Russia would come in, and all agreed that a war with China was senseless since the main arena was still Europe. On November 29, Acheson, trying to make some political capital out of a military disaster, called the Chinese intervention an "act of brazen aggression . . . the second such act in five months. . . . This is not merely another phase of the Korean campaign. This is a fresh and unprovoked aggressive act, even more immoral than the first." [4] That may be exactly what it seemed to Washington but it must be remembered that China for weeks had warned the United States to stay out of North Korea, and that no nation would welcome hostile armies marching up to its very borders.

Even before the Chinese intervention, the Korean War had accelerated a drive in Washington to consider what had

seemed unthinkable to most of the world: a plan to rearm
West Germany. On September 12 Acheson told the un-
believing foreign ministers of Britain and France that Germany must provide ten divisions for NATO. And that month,
partly to try to quiet European fears of a rearmed Germany, the United States sent four divisions to Europe. The
year before, Acheson had reassured the Senate that large
numbers of American troops would not be sent to Europe.
So much had American policy changed in a year.

Just as Korea had alarmed Washington, all this deeply
alarmed Russia. "To the Soviet Union," historian Adam B.
Ulam has written, "West German rearmament was the main
danger to her post-war positions and the prevention of such
a contingency was a principal aim of her foreign policy. In
retrospect, it is not too much to say that a rearmed West
Germany was considered a greater danger than the American
monopoly or superiority in atomic weapons." [5] With this the
American policy shifted even further from the political to
the military, and the Cold War, already a hot war in Asia,
became even more tense in Europe.

As the year ended and the new year, 1951, began, Truman
asked for emergency powers and submitted a $50 billion
defense budget, compared to the $13.5 billion one of six
months before. This set a precedent, and military spending
has spiraled upward ever since.

With American and South Korean armies again fearing
evacuation or complete destruction at the beginning of the
year, the Chinese repeated the mistake the Americans had
made. They, too, saw an opportunity for uniting Korea
under their terms and they pressed forward across the 38th
parallel. But despite some moments of panic in the Ameri-

can army, General Matthew Ridgway, who took command in the field, finally stabilized the situation.

On February 1 the UN General Assembly condemned China as an "aggressor," an action that has enraged China ever since, for China considered the UN, by crossing the 38th parallel, to be the aggressor—which only demonstrates once again that it is always the other side that is the aggressor. There were other important results of the Korean War. The United States reversed itself and began a program of military and economic aid to Chiang Kai-shek. General Marshall said the Communists must never be allowed to take Formosa, Dean Rusk (then an Assistant Secretary of State) said that the United States would recognize Chiang's regime as *the* China, and Acheson said that the United States would attempt to keep Mao's China out of the UN.

During the early months of 1951, MacArthur was prophesying that the American troops would suffer "terrible losses" and even "be driven off the peninsula" unless Truman followed his recommendations: 1. blockade the Chinese coast; 2. bomb China itself; 3. get Nationalist troops from Formosa to fight in Korea; 4. assist Chiang's troops to make diversionary raids on vulnerable areas of China. This, of course, would have meant all-out war against China with incalculable consequences. Finally, when it became clear that MacArthur simply would not follow orders from Washington, he was fired on April 11 by Truman with the complete concurrence of the Joint Chiefs of Staff.

The American reaction was incredible. MacArthur, who defied civilian authority, became a national hero unlike any in American history. In Congress there was a movement to impeach Truman, Marshall, and Acheson. The White House received 78,000 telegrams running 20 to 1 against the dismissal, and a Gallup Poll said only 29 per cent of the people supported Truman's action. MacArthur got a wild ticker-tape parade up Broadway and made an unprecedented appearance before a joint session of Congress. But despite the extraordinary dimensions of the uproar, it eventually faded away and Truman successfully defended the vital principle of civilian supremacy over the military.

On the battlefield, Ridgway rallied his forces, stemmed the Chinese and North Korean troops, and then took the offensive once more. By March, after a winter campaign fought in bitter cold, with icy winds as much the enemy as the Chinese and North Koreans, the allies had regained the 38th parallel but could not drive much farther north. A classic military stalemate had developed. When the Chinese pushed south, their fragile supply lines became too vulnerable to American air power. When the allies pushed north, the Chinese supply lines were shortened and they could blunt any offensive by sheer weight of manpower. Thus, on June 30, Ridgway broadcast to the Communists that the United States was willing to discuss an armistice. Two days later Kim Il Sung agreed and talks began on July 8.

There was to be no quick settlement, though, and while the talks dragged on endlessly, bitter positional fighting took place, costing tens of thousands of lives on both sides until an armistice was finally signed on July 27, 1953. It was during these frustrating and anguished days that McCarthyism flourished as never before, causing the rest of the world to shake its head in amazement at the convulsions that sometimes seemed on the verge of ripping apart the fabric of American society.

The Korean War had still another tragic consequence for the United States. At the end of World War II, American sympathies had been with the rebels in Indochina, and Washington repeatedly urged France to drop its imperialistic effort to retain its grip on the rice-rich peninsula. But France was not yet ready to see its imperial glories wane and tried to suppress by force of arms Ho Chi Minh's Vietminh. The United States at first stayed out of this conflict, but after China went to the Communists and the Korean War began, the French role began to change in Washington's eyes from a struggle to retain empire to a valiant effort to stop the spread of Communism. America started to give economic aid to help pay for the French campaign in Indochina. It began with $150 million and by 1954 when the French effort collapsed, it had reached $1 billion a year, about a third of America's foreign aid expenditures.

September 1951 saw the Japanese Peace Treaty, negotiated by John Foster Dulles, who was soon to become President Eisenhower's Secretary of State. By terms of the treaty, Japan allowed American military bases and men on its soil and it was given—over the objections of many Japanese—the right to rearm. Again the United States reversed its policy, for earlier, under MacArthur's consulship, Japan's new constitution had embodied a prohibition against rearming.[6]

Dulles also negotiated a series of mutual defense treaties with the Philippines, New Zealand, and Australia, another reversal of American policy, for Acheson during the NATO hearings had assured the Senators that the North Atlantic alliance would not be the first of a series the world over. But now the United States, seeing the Communist menace as world-wide, acted accordingly.

In 1952 Acheson tried to get final agreement from Britain and France for a rearmed Germany. But they were reluctant; they had not forgotten the cruel punishment they had suffered at German hands, so Acheson often found himself agreeing with Konrad Adenauer, Chancellor (Prime Minister) of West Germany, a former enemy, and disagreeing with two old allies.

That March the Truman Administration had its last chance to seek a lessening of Cold War tension. Russia made a staggering offer. It proposed a German peace treaty that would make that nation united and independent. It would permit Germany a national army tied to neither East nor West, provide for the withdrawal of all foreign troops from Germany and for its admission to the United Nations. This proposal may have been mere propaganda but we will never know, since Acheson simply refused to discuss it. Perhaps he believed there was no chance to tone down the Cold War and that even talking about it would weaken Western determination to increase its military strength. Whether this was the case or not, what may have been a major opportunity for a reduction of Cold War tensions was lost, for soon the United States became involved in a Presidential election and under the Republican winners, attitudes would harden even further.

In late May the United States, Britain, and France ended the occupation of Germany in their three zones. With that action went the last good chance to negotiate with Russia a German peace treaty which even today has yet to be signed. But the West was convinced that its economic, political, and military strength depended on integrating into its camp the strengths of West Germany.

Also that month John Foster Dulles pronounced his famous doctrine of "massive retaliation." The soon-to-be Secretary of State said the United States must have "the will and . . . the means to retaliate instantly against open aggression by Red armies so that, if it occurred anywhere, we could and would strike back where it hurts, by means of our own choosing."

William G. Carleton describes the reaction of America's allies:

This new strategy stirred the gravest misgivings. . . . Who would do the choosing as to when and where [a nuclear weapon] was to be used? Would America's allies be consulted? How about humanitarian considerations? Was every little war to be turned into a nuclear holocaust? [7]

In the first place, few in Western Europe expected a direct Russian assault. Apart from the fact that such an attack would almost surely result in a nuclear response from the United States, there were few who believed that Russia would take such an extreme step even if there were no nuclear threat. It seemed clear by 1952 that whatever Russia's ambitions were, they would be sought by nonmilitary means, at least in Europe.

Further, there was the fear—and this increased after the Eisenhower Administration took office—that undue reliance on nuclear retaliation, although certainly cheaper than building up substantial conventional forces, would weaken the American ability to respond to "brushfire" wars too small to justify a nuclear response. Also, such tough talk did nothing to lessen Russian fears of American intentions.

The 1952 election, which saw the great military hero of

World War II, five-star General Dwight D. Eisenhower, run against the Governor of Illinois, Adlai E. Stevenson, was in some ways similar to that of 1968.[8] Harry S. Truman, like Lyndon B. Johnson, decided not to run for re-election, influenced no doubt by the unpopularity of the Korean War. There were, however, other factors as well: the feeling that it was "time for a change" after twenty straight years of Democratic rule, and the issue of Communism generally, with many Americans persuaded that Harry Truman who had put the United States on a Cold War footing was "soft on Communism," a charge widely believed despite its obvious absurdity.

The Republicans exploited this feeling, with General Eisenhower promising to "go to Korea" to end the war, and with Dulles promising "to roll back the Iron Curtain" and "liberate" the captive nations. The first was possible, the second, as the Hungarian Revolution of 1956 was to make tragically plain, was not. Eisenhower scored a landslide victory over Stevenson who, nonetheless, captured the allegiance of millions with his eloquence and his practice of "talking sense" to the American people.

If there was no easing of pressure on the American side of the Cold War, neither was there on the Russian side. Late in 1952 and early the following year the aging Stalin pushed a hard line, calling for "a fierce struggle against the enemy."

8

The Dulles Crusade

Some students of recent history have long regarded the Cold War as a series of missed opportunities on both sides. 1953 certainly was such a year for the Americans.

Less than two months after the Eisenhower Administration took office Josef Stalin died. For the first time in nearly three decades Russia was free of the brutal hand of one of the strongest figures of modern history. Crafty, sometimes cautious, sometimes bold to the point of recklessness, ruthless and cold-blooded yet passionately devoted to Russia, darkly suspicious, perhaps even paranoiac, few tyrants in all history have held so much power for so long or have so changed the course of events. Stalin led his nation from a struggling backward country to one of the two great powers of the world—but at what a cost. Brutal purges that took the lives of hundreds of thousands, perhaps millions; a repressive, closed society that still, more than a decade and a half after Stalin's death, has made little progress toward liberty; a foreign policy that has imposed repressive societies on most of its neighbors for nearly a quarter of a century.

Stalin's death presented an extraordinary opportunity to lessen the tensions of the Cold War. Shortly thereafter, Georgi Malenkov, Stalin's first successor, said, "At the present time there is no dispute or unresolved question that cannot be settled peacefully by mutual agreement of the interested countries. This applies to our relations with all states, including the United States of America." The Kremlin's new leaders gave proof of the change by permitting "Russians married to foreigners to leave the country, reestablishing diplomatic relations with Greece, Israel, and later Yugoslavia, withdrawing former objections to the appointment of a new Secretary-General of the United Nations, renouncing Soviet claims to Turkish territory, and, most important, agreeing to an end to the Korean War." [1]

The time seemed right for a change on the American side too, for the Truman Administration, which had taken a hard line on the Cold War, had given way to the Eisenhower Administration. But the new American Secretary of State, John Foster Dulles, was even more rigid on the question of Communism than his predecessor, Dean Acheson. Dulles, strong-willed and highly moralistic, saw the Cold War as a clear struggle between good and evil and his influence on President Eisenhower was so great that his views dominated American foreign policy. In January he had told the Senate Foreign Relations Committee reviewing his nomination that the competition between the United States and the Soviet Union was "an irreconcilable conflict." Then on April 16 Eisenhower made a formal reply to Malenkov, saying that if Russia really wanted an easing of tensions, it must make a series of concessions in Korea, Southeast Asia, Germany, and Eastern Europe. The following day Dulles issued a statement that the *New York Times* headlined "Dulles Bids Soviets Cooperate or Face Vast West Arming." The United States had decided that this was not the time for negotiations with Russia. It was still engaged in war in Korea; it still viewed the world situation in terms of a Sino-Soviet conspiracy.

But even that life-long anti-Communist, Winston Churchill, thought that the aftermath of Stalin's death was a time to seek a lessening of tensions. On May 11 he called, in effect, for a summit conference and suggested that the world's problems be tackled one by one, instead of trying to solve them all at once as Eisenhower had demanded. The British leader also said it was necessary to assure Russian security. The United States was as cool to Churchill's proposals as it had been to Malenkov's.

If Stalin's death did not have any immediate effect on Russo-American relations, it did have a prophetic effect within the Russian Empire. The new rulers relaxed somewhat their grip on the satellites, and this encouraged the people of East Germany to seek even further liberalization. Workers marched down Stalinallee in East Berlin and the next day the protests spread, with workers tearing down Communist banners and demanding free elections. The American radio in West Berlin applauded the East German workers, but when Russian tanks appeared in a number of cities to put down the demonstrations, Dulles, who had called for the "liberation" of Eastern Europe, took no action. This foreshadowed what was to happen in Budapest three years later.

Although there was little progress in Europe, the war in

Korea was at last brought to an end. Some have said that the Communists finally, after two frustrating years, engaged in fruitful negotiations because of an exercise in Dulles diplomacy that came to be known as "brinkmanship": going to the brink of nuclear war to convince your opponents that you mean business. On May 22 Dulles hinted to Peking through Indian diplomats—the same channel China had used without effect three years before—that the United States might use atomic weapons if there were not a settlement soon. Whatever the reason—perhaps the Chinese and North Koreans were influenced by Dulles' hints; perhaps they, too, had tired of the long, bloody, and inconclusive war—agreement was reached at the truce village of Panmunjom and an armistice signed on July 27.

The armistice did end the bloodshed, but it was a triumph for neither side. On the debit side for the Communists, the North Koreans and Chinese had suffered staggering losses; the United States had interposed itself between Formosa and mainland China, postponing for decades, perhaps forever, the Chinese expectation of regaining that island; and China was forced by the United States into a diplomatic and economic isolation that was to last for a decade or more. On the debit side for the United States, while the war had prevented the North Koreans from conquering South Korea, it also had failed to unite Korea by force, had given China a chance to prove that it was a military power, and tensions between the giant nations had unsettled conditions in Asia for decades. Not least, of course, was the loss of more than 30,000 American dead in the war. Nor was there accomplished even a stable settlement in Korea. Skirmishing has continued along the armistice line ever since, and in recent years both sides have accused the other of infiltration, with tension reaching a high point in January 1968 when North Korea seized the U.S.S. *Pueblo,* an intelligence ship, claiming it was within its territorial waters.

Although there were no other major Cold War developments in the second half of 1953, there were some straws in the wind. On July 26 an obscure Cuban revolutionary, 26-year-old Fidel Castro, and his younger brother, Raul, led 165 youths in an abortive attack on an army barracks in Santiago, Cuba. Half of the rebels fell before army machine-gun fire but the Castro brothers escaped and fled to Mexico. There they began the 26th of July Movement which within six years would take them to the Sierra Maestra and, after guerrilla warfare from the mountains, in triumph to Havana, toppling the dictatorship of American-supported Fulgencio Batista.

Seemingly unrelated, there was another development that summer which further demonstrated that the Cold War, begun along the tense line dividing East and West in Europe, would actually be fought far away in Asia, the Middle East, and even in America's traditional preserve, Latin America. Sometimes the struggle would be open as in the Dominican Republic and Vietnam. More often it would be clandestine as it was that August in Iran when Kermit Roosevelt, grandson of President Theodore Roosevelt, led a coup planned, financed, and executed by the Central Intelligence Agency that toppled the nationalist leader, Premier Mohammed Mossadeq.[2]

Although the State Department hinted there were ties between Mossadeq and the Communists, they were actually bitter rivals. Mossadeq had put down Communist demonstrations with force and refused their aid even when Ameri-

can efforts to topple him became transparent. With Mossadeq
jailed, power was returned to the Shah (King), American aid
poured in, American oil companies broke the British monopoly, and, in 1955, Iran joined the Baghdad Pact, the Ameri-
can-sponsored alliance in the Middle East.

Of the CIA, Richard J. Barnet has written:

Most of their activities, however, have been directed against regimes which have tried to take a radical or nationalist position
on questions of development and foreign policy. Such regimes
have attempted to nationalize foreign enterprises, have flirted
with Marxist rhetoric, or have invited persons with real or sus-
pected Communist associations into the government. Any of these
deviations from the standard which the United States has set for
judging whether a foreign government is a responsible member of
the Free World has been sufficient to convince the State Department that the government in question is "subverted" and that
it is fair game for "counter-subversive" operations from our side.
While on occasion CIA agents may act prematurely and display
too much zeal, and even sometimes, as in Laos in 1960, may act
counter to official State Department policy at that moment, in
most cases the agency is carrying out official policy that has been
approved by the President. Subversion is simply another facet of
the campaign against revolution. It is a technique which is
cheaper and politically less embarrassing than open support of
one side in a protracted civil war or landing American troops.[3]

Although Barnet's views are shared by an increasing number of writers and historians, there are still those in government and out who would argue that leftist governments
anywhere in the world are a threat to America's political,
economic, and military interests and that therefore the United
States has a right, the right of self-defense, to intervene in

their domestic affairs. This, of course, is a basic question. Does the United States—or Russia or any other nation—have the right to interfere in the internal matters of another country and, if so, when and under what circumstances?

1953 saw yet another example of Dulles' conviction that the West must strengthen itself militarily. In September the United States and the Fascist dictator, Francisco Franco, signed an agreement allowing American bases to be established in Spain. In return for the airfields and naval bases, Franco got large amounts of financial assistance. Although Dulles explained the pact as being a military necessity, it aroused wide protests in the United States and Europe.

Dulles made further commitments in 1954 which would affect the course of American history for years to come. The move toward these commitments was not evident at first, for in a February press conference, President Eisenhower said of Southeast Asia, "I cannot conceive of a greater tragedy for America than to get heavily involved now in an all-out war in any of these regions, particularly with large units." He was, of course, reflecting the current determination of most American military men not to get entangled in a land war on the Asian mainland. They had learned from Korea that the logistic and tactical problems were immense and they were not eager to repeat that bitter and frustrating experience.

But by March Eisenhower had started to modify his position. As the French hold on Indochina began to collapse, General Paul Ely, French Chief of Staff, flew to Washington and told Eisenhower that disaster was imminent unless the United States intervened immediately. Despite enormous amounts of American aid in money and military equipment, despite the expenditure of cruel numbers of French fighting

men, particularly officers, the French were on the verge of
defeat. They had staked everything on the defense of Dienbienphu, which has given its name to one of the most significant battles in modern history.

General Henri Navarre, the French commander in Indochina, decided his last chance was to draw Ho Chi Minh's
swelling forces into a conventional pitched battle and destroy
them with massed artillery. An interlocking chain of for-
tresses was constructed, defended by artillery quite superior,
the French thought, to any available to the Vietminh. The
Vietminh, under the command of the great guerrilla fighter,
General Vo Nguyen Giap, accepted the challenge but the
French were tragically wrong about the Vietminh artillery.
Somehow they managed to drag heavy pieces across the mountains and the French, now a fixed target, found themselves
outgunned.

Ely pleaded with Washington to intervene. He found
sympathetic listeners. Admiral Arthur Radford, Chairman of
the Joint Chiefs, was ready to go, as was Vice President
Richard M. Nixon and other powerful voices in the Administration, including, more cautiously, Dulles. Eisenhower was
sympathetic but even more cautious. He knew the French had
antagonized most of the Vietnamese population and that Ho
Chi Minh was a national hero. Nonetheless, Eisenhower was
prepared to intervene then if he could get support, even
token support, from allied nations and from the Congress.

Neither was forthcoming. The British didn't think intervention at so late an hour would be effective; it feared it
would defeat any chance for a political settlement and might
even cause a general war in Asia. And Congress, which had

been so bitterly critical of the Korean War, was not prepared to engage in another just a year later.[4]

Dienbienphu fell on May 7, the day before the Geneva Conference began discussing the Indochina question. The conference had actually begun on April 26 with talks on Korea, but it soon became clear no progress would be made on that question and on May 8 it took up Indochina. The French were ready for a settlement, for Vietnam had affected that nation as it would the United States more than a decade later. The war had taken a heavy toll of French lives, but even more telling was its domestic effect on the people of France. They had wearied of the war and there was widespread disaffection. The French wanted the war to end. Prime Minister Joseph Laniel fell on the issue—much as Lyndon Johnson was to fall in 1968—and his successor, Pierre Mendes-France, declared that if there were not a satisfactory settlement by July 20, he would resign.

Agreement was reached by July 20, one that the Vietminh was not entirely happy about. Evidently in response to pressure from mainland China and Russia, they conceded more than they thought they should in view of their dominant position on the battlefield. The two Communist giants evidently feared that unsuccessful negotiations would strengthen the hands of those Americans who wanted to intervene militarily. So the Vietminh compromised, confident that the forthcoming elections provided for in the agreement would make their victory complete.

According to the Geneva Agreements, the 17th parallel was established as a temporary demarcation line and the Vietminh would withdraw its troops from the vast areas it

controlled south of that line, pending the nation's reunification after countrywide elections to be held in July 1956.
There were these important provisions:

A group of four articles in the armistice pact provided for the
insulation of Vietnam from the international pressures of the
Cold War. Article 16 banned the introduction into the whole
of Vietnam, North and South, of "any troop reinforcements and
additional military personnel" from the outside. Article 17
banned "the introduction into Vietnam of any reinforcements in
the form of all types of arms, munitions and other war matériel,
such as combat aircraft, naval craft, pieces of ordnance, jet en-
gines and jet weapons, and armoured vehicles." Article 18 forbade
the establishment of "new military bases." The purpose of Article
19 was the neutralization of all of Vietnam. It stated: "No military base under the control of a foreign State may be established
in the regrouping zone of either party; the two parties shall
ensure that the zones assigned to them do not adhere to any military alliance and are not used for the resumption of military
hostilities or to further an aggressive policy." [5]

　　The United States did not sign the Geneva Agreements,
but it "took note" of them and "declared" that the United
States would "refrain from the threat or the use of force to
disturb them." Yet while the United States in this way ap-
parently recognized the agreements, its critics have charged
that it violated all four of the above provisions by giving military aid to the South Vietnamese regime of Ngo Dinh Diem,
the increasingly dictatorial ruler.

　　The United States has long referred to South Vietnam as a
sovereign state and termed the acts of the indigenous Viet
Cong and later the North Vietnamese as "aggression." But
the language of the Final Declaration of July 21, 1954 is abso-

lutely explicit on this point. "The Conference recognizes that the essential purpose of the agreement relating to Viet Nam is to settle military questions with a view to ending hostilities *and that the military demarcation line is provisional and should not in any way be interpreted as constituting a political or territorial boundary* [italics mine]." Thus, it is clear that North and South Vietnam are part of one country and that any war within that nation is a civil war, not an international war; there is no question of external aggression.

Dulles liked the Geneva Agreements even less than did the Vietminh and he immediately took steps to counter their effects. On September 8 the Southeast Asia Treaty Organization (SEATO) was established in Manila by the United States, Britain, France, Australia, New Zealand, Thailand, Pakistan, and the Philippines. Cambodia, Laos, and the southern part of Vietnam were included by means of a protocol. The formation of SEATO may not have violated the letter of the Geneva Agreements, but as Kahin and Lewis so firmly state in *The United States in Vietnam,* "It clearly violated their spirit, both by implying that the 17th parallel had a political character and by its inconsistency with the neutral status of the southern regroupment zone. At the very least its provisions signalled the American intent to underwrite a separate state in southern Vietnam if, despite the inadmissibility of this under the Geneva Agreements, one could be established." [6]

While the Indochina talks were going on in Geneva, there was an interesting incident in Guatemala. Although in terms of American foreign policy it was only a minor incident, it did affect the future course of history for that tiny Central

American nation. The background is confusing, but the elected President, Jacobo Arbenz Guzmán, was accused by the United States of accepting local Communists as "an authentic domestic political party." There seems little doubt that Arbenz did have some Guatemalan Communists in high places, some of whom took direction from Moscow. Yet according to Richard Barnet, and other historians concur, "Guatemala was far from adopting a Communist economy or social system. She was receiving no aid from the Soviet Union or indeed had any relationship with the Communist bloc. Arbenz was actually using the Communists to help administer a continuation of the moderate reformist program of (former President) Arevalo, who was a rather strong anti-Communist." [7]

The Eisenhower Administration decided that Arbenz had to go, and the CIA chose Colonel Castillo Armas to succeed him. The CIA established training bases in Honduras and Nicaragua, and on June 18 Armas led 150 exile mercenaries into Guatemala while American pilots bombed the capital. The army, which could have crushed the exile force, refused to support Arbenz, partly because his reforms had not yet produced results, partly because they did not want to oppose the Americans. The CIA coup succeeded and Dulles reported to the American people that the situation was "being cured by the Guatemalans themselves."

With the overthrow of Arbenz, the United Fruit Company regained expropriated lands and certain taxes were abolished, saving that American firm about $11 million. The United States poured American military and economic aid into Guatemala but, as was the case in Greece, even massive American intervention was not able to stabilize the country. Fourteen years later politics by violence was still the rule in Guatemala, and in 1968 the American Ambassador, John Gordon Mein, and two embassy aides, were slain in two separate incidents, reportedly as acts of retaliation in the continuing struggle between the government and pro-Communist rebels, with brutalities on both sides.

Despite these 1954 developments in Indochina and Guatemala, Europe was still the main arena as far as the United States was concerned. In August, Tito's Yugoslavia joined Greece and Turkey in a Balkan alliance, and since the latter two countries had been added to NATO, Communist Yugoslavia also became in a way associated with it. There was a temporary defeat for Dulles in August when the French Parliament refused to ratify that nation's adherence to the European Defense Community, an organization that was to have been the means of getting a rearmed Germany into the Western alliance. The French still feared a German army.

Dulles said the French rejection had caused "a crisis of almost terrifying proportions." But he was determined to have a rearmed Germany, and a way was devised to overcome French objections. Britain and the United States both made long-term commitments of troops to Europe, helping to quiet French fears that a German army would become dominant in Western Europe. Thus, the Western European Union was enlarged to include West Germany and German troops would soon join NATO through the back door.

The year 1954 ended as it began, with attention focused on Asia. In December the United States and Nationalist China signed a Mutual Defense Treaty by which the United States guaranteed the security of Formosa. In return Chiang Kai-shek pledged not to attack the mainland (something beyond his capability in any case) nor to reinforce the offshore islands without American consent.

Contradictory trends set in in 1955. That year saw the emergence of Nikita Khrushchev as the Kremlin's leader. He undertook an international campaign to convince the world of Russia's dedication to "peaceful coexistence," its determination to carry out the spread of Communism by peaceful methods. At the same time Russia began to aid revolutionary movements in the Middle East and Asia, a policy that was bound to alarm Washington even though there was never any evidence that Moscow dominated any of these movements.

There were also contradictory directions in Washington's policy. On the one hand, with the signing of the Baghdad Pact in February, Dulles completed his ring of alliances around the Communist world. "The purpose of the pact," he said, "is not in any way to disrupt the Arab world" but to stabilize the Middle East and ". . . to create a solid band of resistance against the Soviet Union." Britain, Turkey, Iraq, Iran, and Pakistan formed the pact. The United States, although its sponsor, was not a member; it was already allied to all five nations by one treaty or another. On the other hand, Eisenhower at a summit meeting in Geneva in July established pleasant relations with the Russian leaders, causing a relaxation of tensions that the now public-relations-conscious Russians liked to call "the Spirit of Geneva."

Dulles believed that the Russian conciliatory attitude was in response to the firm line taken by the United States. The line was firm indeed. In January 1955, following the shelling of Quemoy and Matsu, two Nationalist-held islands just nine miles off the Chinese mainland, tension increased between China and the United States. Eisenhower went to Congress and demanded what has been termed a "blank check" resolution, empowering him to use American forces to defend the Nationalists. He got the resolution with only a total of six votes against it in both houses of Congress. This precedent was to be recalled by Lyndon Johnson, in 1955 Senate Majority Leader, during the Tonkin Gulf crisis in 1964 when he was President. But the 1955 crisis simply faded away.

In May, West German armies were formally admitted into NATO, with West Germany and Italy joining the Western alliance. With this, Britain, France, and the United States formally ended the occupation of West Germany which then regained its sovereignty. Two important declarations were appended to this Paris Pact. John Spanier summarizes them:

In the first, the West German Government subscribed to the principles of the United Nations, recognized the defensive nature of the Brussels and NATO treaties, undertook "never to have recourse to force to achieve the reunification of Germany or the modification of the present boundaries of the German Federal Republic," and to resolve all disputes between herself and other states by peaceful means. In the second, the United States, Britain, and France declared that they recognized the Federal Republic as the only freely and legitimately constituted government entitled to speak for all of Germany; that they would pursue German reunification by peaceful means; and that they would continue to exercise their responsibilities with regard to the security of West Germany and West Berlin.[8]

Thus, another milestone in postwar history was passed. The bigger and more important part of Germany was now firmly in the Western alliance and in return it had regained its sovereignty. But there was a price: the indefinite division of Germany and continued Cold War tension. On May 5 the Russians, fearful of a remilitarized West Germany, joined Albania, Bulgaria, Czechoslovakia, East Germany, Hungary, Poland, and Rumania in signing the Warsaw Pact, a mutual defense treaty which was to be the Soviet bloc's equivalent of NATO.

Later in May, the Austrian State Treaty was signed at Vienna. This treaty restored Austria to full sovereignty on the condition that it become allied with neither side in the Cold War and allow no foreign military bases on its soil. It led to the prompt withdrawal of Russian troops, ending its farthest penetration into Central Europe. Why had the Soviets agreed to this and at this time? According to one historian, William G. Carleton:

The Russians meant this treaty to be both a warning and a promise to Germany. The Russians, in effect, were saying to the West Germans: "You see, Austria did not join either side, and now Austria is unified and freed from all foreign occupation. If you West Germans had remained neutral, if you had not joined the West, you, too, might have been reunited with your fellow nationals in the East and your soil cleared of foreign occupation. You West Germans had better reconsider your alliance with the Western powers and your rearmament program, if you want to achieve national reunification." [9]

There is considerable validity to this, yet there is no doubt that Germany was vastly more important to both sides in the Cold War and that it was much easier to make mutual concessions on powerless Austria.

The Austrian State Treaty was not the only sign of Russian mellowing in 1955. That year Khrushchev journeyed to Belgrade to apologize to Tito and to proclaim that there were "separate roads to socialism," although Khrushchev himself in 1956 (Hungary) and his successors in 1968 (Czechoslovakia) evidently did not feel bound by this pronouncement. Also in 1955 Russia returned to China its naval base at Port Arthur, recognized West Germany, sought to "normalize" its relations with Turkey, and relinquished its naval and military bases at Porkkala, Finland. Now Khrushchev could say that Russia no longer had military bases on foreign soil. Of course, he continued to define Russian troops in the satellite nations as members of a joint defense force.

That year China was also following a peaceful line compared to the bellicose words (but cautious actions) that would characterize its behavior in succeeding years. Premier Chou En-lai had gone to the Bandung Conference of nonaligned states in April "charming his fellow delegates from Asia and Africa by the moderation and breadth of his views and his forcible renunciation of any idea of exporting revolution. China, he declared, was ready to talk with the United States about a peaceful solution of the Formosa question, why she was not even averse to talking with the Nationalist Chinese about a peaceful and decorous way of taking them over." [10]

9

That Incredible Year

1956 BEGAN with dramatic change and ended with both East and West badly shaken by the year's events.

The Communist world was first to feel the tremors. They began when Khrushchev shocked his Communist brothers in late February. An incredulous audience at the 20th Party Congress in Moscow heard Khrushchev accuse Stalin of crimes against the Russian people and the Communist party. It was unbelievable. They all knew of Stalin's brutality and cruelty, of course—many of them had suffered from it. But it was something never to be mentioned publicly, a necessary price to be paid, for Stalin had been the unchallengeable fountainhead of latter-day Communism. To attack him was to attack Communism itself.

However, Khrushchev, not without courage, had decided that the day of Stalinism was over (although he and all his top colleagues had assisted Stalin in his crimes), that the times had changed, and that Russia must change with them. Khrushchev thought it was necessary that a degree of liberalization take place within the Soviet Union and its empire. He knew he was taking a risk, an unacceptable risk according to many in the Kremlin, but his wishes prevailed.

To understand the extraordinary results of Khrushchev's new policy, it is necessary to look at the Eastern Europe of 1956. In Russia itself, although there was some internal pressure for liberalization, Communism and nationalism were essentially the same thing. Thus there was no tension between them. This was not so, though, in the satellites. Although the other countries may have accepted Russian leadership and may even have been convinced Communists, they wanted their own kind of Communism, one that reflected their cultures and national aspirations. The people were restless; they wanted to establish their own national identities. But the leaders imposed on them by Stalin were nervous. They were afraid that if they relaxed their grip even a bit, they might lose control. They were right, for in human affairs explosions come not when the pressure is greatest but when it has begun to lessen: the racial difficulties in the United States in the late 1960's are a perfect demonstration.

The first signs of the growing tensions in Eastern Europe became visible in Poland in June. "It found its most violent expression," Adam B. Ulam relates, "among the youth and the intelligentsia, followed at a safe distance by Party functionaries, but it eventually spread to the people at large. In June, in the major Polish city of Poznan, an industrial strike turned into a national revolt, with the offices of the secret police and local party organs being attacked and sacked. The Polish government had to have recourse to the use of armed forces, who extinguished the uprising, but the reaction of the soldiers was most alarming." [1]

The Kremlin was indeed alarmed and sent top leaders to an urgent meeting of the Polish Central Committee. It was decided to bring back to the committee the party's former Secretary-General, Wladyslaw Gomulka, who had been expelled and imprisoned for alleged Titoism. But Gomulka refused to be exploited and held out for, and got, his old job. Despite the protests of some hard-liners (they exist on both sides of the Iron Curtain), the Polish party decided some internal reforms were essential to avoid a widespread revolt.

These were nervous days for Khrushchev and his supporters. They didn't want to go back to old Stalin-type repression but were afraid of uncontrolled liberalism. And what would the American response be to repression—remember, Dulles was still talking about "roll back" and "liberation"—to Soviet troops putting down a rebellion in one of the satellites?

Finally, an ironic course was chosen. Tito, once condemned as a heretic, began to be hailed as an example of a leader who could be both a loyal Communist and a nationalist. His advice and company were fervently sought and he counseled moderation both in the Kremlin and the satellites. The big trouble was that there were few Titos in those capitals.

Worse than Poznan, much worse, was yet to come. Before that, however, the other great drama of 1956 was emerging. In June Dulles made another of his famous pronouncements, that neutrality was "an immoral and short-sighted conception." In brief, those nations that were not with us were against us. This philosophy contributed to a decision regarding the Middle East that would have profound repercussions throughout the world. The background is terribly complex, involving Arab-Israeli relations, Cold War considerations, and U.S. domestic political and economic concerns. But in short, Gamal Abdel Nasser of Egypt wanted to buy arms to strengthen his nation relative to Israel. He approached the West and was given a price that was immediately undercut by the Communists who wished to increase their influence in the area and undermine Eisenhower's Baghdad Pact. This Communist move caused Dulles to make a countermove. He offered to help Nasser pay for the huge and immensely expensive Aswan Dam that was to be Nasser's great achievement. Dulles evidently figured that Nasser could not afford both the Aswan Dam and Czech arms.[2]

However, Dulles got more deeply involved than he had bargained for. At home his move drew sharp criticism. Nasser had dropped his recognition of Chiang Kai-shek and in May recognized Mao Tse-tung's Communist government in China. This enraged the China Lobby in America who joined those supporting Israel in opposing Dulles' offer to Nasser. And then, to make things worse, Egypt decided to go ahead with the Czech arms deal. Dulles, under strong pressure and believing that Russia could not afford to finance the Aswan Dam, decided to reverse his field. In mid-July he withdrew his offer to Nasser, striking what he figured would be a disastrous blow to the Egyptian leader who had staked so much on the dam.

Nasser struck back a week later by seizing the British-controlled Suez Canal. This bold stroke brought the Arab leader great respect in the Middle East. It also alarmed Britain, to whom Suez was not only a vital lifeline but the symbol of British prestige in an area she had long dominated. Thus, Dulles' action set the stage for the Suez crisis that fall and, ironically, cleared the way for the gradual strengthening of

Soviet influence in the Middle East. For, afford it or not, Khrushchev did help Nasser build the Aswan Dam, and Russia has been a major factor in the area ever since.

There was another event in mid-1956, perhaps not important in itself, but indicative of the thinking of Eisenhower's Republican party. As it prepared for the fall election in which Eisenhower would again meet Adlai Stevenson, the Republicans in their party platform called for ". . . the establishment of American bases strategically dispersed all around the world." This again demonstrated how profoundly the Soviet Union and the United States misunderstood each other. The United States had established bases all over the world, and its young men were stationed thousands of miles from home, because it feared Communist aggression. On the other hand, Russia interpreted these bases, many of them airfields for strategic bombers that could carry nuclear weapons to Russia's heartland, as the hostile encirclement by capitalists it had always feared.

Meanwhile, further symptoms of unrest appeared in Poland. Alarmed that the Poles were liberalizing too fast, an imposing Russian delegation—including Khrushchev and Molotov—flew to Warsaw in October and Russian troops began to converge on the Polish border from two directions. But Gomulka, backed by even the Stalinists in his party, stood up to the Russians and even threatened to distribute weapons to Polish workers. The Russians, convinced the Poles meant business, backed down. The last thing Khrushchev wanted was an armed confrontation between those ancient enemies, Russians and Poles.

However, it must be made clear that Gomulka was no heretic. He was a loyal Communist. Further, he remembered

German savagery during the war and he recognized that Poland could not stand alone against a rearmed Germany that would inevitably demand back the land it had lost to Poland after the war. Nor could it resist Russian might. But Gomulka was also a Polish nationalist and he has been engaged in an extraordinary balancing act ever since.

The word of the Poles' astounding success in facing down the Russians spread through the Communist world and had immediate and eventually brutal consequences in Hungary. The volatile Hungarians, eager for freedom, erupted. A story of incredible bravery, no less noble for its futility, was about to unfold.

John Lukacs describes the beginnings of the uprising this way:

During the first three weeks of October, symbolic reforms and significant events in Budapest assumed a trend that was somewhat similar to that of Warsaw. But, even though events in Budapest were touched off by the news from Warsaw, in Hungary, unlike in Poland, a domestic revolution broke out on 23 October. On that day, when [the hated Russian-appointed Prime Minister] Gero was still on his way back from a state visit to Belgrade, an almost spontaneous demonstration started by university students pulled the people of Budapest into the streets and squares by evening. A large crowd of demonstrators appeared in Parliament Square, demanding [the former Prime Minister] Imre Nagy. A hasty, stupid and snarling radio address by Gero had the worst possible effects for the regime. Meanwhile demonstrators were besieging the building of the Magyar Radio, where the secret police opened fire. By that time workers from the industrial outskirts of Budapest were arriving in trucks, carrying a variety of weapons. Stalin's gigantic statue, erected on the site of a Catholic church only a few years before, was destroyed amidst

frenzied scenes of jubilation and dragged into the center of the
city. Through the night demonstrations, attacks on Communist
press headquarters, and rifle fire went on.[3]

The next day the world awoke to hear that a spontaneous
revolution was sweeping across Hungary. The army, the
police, workers' organizations, almost everyone was joining
the rebels. The Communist government was in a panic. It
broadcast promises mixed with threats. It announced the re-
appointment of the more liberal Imre Nagy as Premier, but
it was too late. The fire had been ignited. The regime called
on Russian tanks to enter Budapest to restore order. They
did, cautiously, and some were set ablaze, but the great toll
of Hungarian patriots was taken not by Russian guns but by
those of the hated secret police who were fighting for their
lives.

On the 24th or 25th two top Russians, Anastas Mikoyan
and Mikhail Suslov, flew to Budapest at some risk and were
taken to Communist party headquarters in Soviet armored
cars. They decided to support Nagy and the unpopular Gero
was spirited away. But by now Nagy himself had become
infected by the revolution and he proclaimed that Hungary
would withdraw from the Warsaw Pact and become a neutral
nation.

This may have been fatal, for Nagy, unlike Gomulka, got
carried away. For a while, however, it seemed as if he had
triumphed, for on October 28 the Russian tanks began to
withdraw from Budapest. On the 30th Mikoyan and Suslov
again flew to Budapest to take a first-hand look at the fluid
situation.

On that day a long Moscow communiqué of extraordinary significance announced the withdrawal of Russian troops from all of Budapest and eventually from Hungary; more important, it suggested not only support to the Nagy government but a fundamental revision of the relations of Russia with her Eastern European "socialist" neighbor states under the Warsaw Pact.[4]

On that fateful day it seemed as if the Soviet Empire were crumbling, that Communism had succumbed to nationalism and that the leaders of the Kremlin were standing by helplessly. But tragically, the story was not yet over; the heroism of the Hungarian patriots was not to be crowned with freedom.

On October 31 the leaders of the Russian Empire met in the Kremlin. We may never know what was said, or to what degree, if any, events in the Middle East influenced the Russian decision, but we do know what followed. That night Russian tank columns leaving Hungary stopped and turned around. Khrushchev and the other leaders had decided that whatever the cost, the Hungarian revolution must be crushed.

The decision could not have been easy because the Russians were aware that the sympathy of almost the entire world lay with the Hungarians. They must also have been concerned about what the Americans might do. Nonetheless, the decision was made and it was carried out unflinchingly, despite the condemnation of the United Nations and the outrage of people the world over.

Brutally, systematically, the Russians put down the revolution. Still, for two more weeks, Hungarian patriots fought on. But courage was no match for tanks, and soon a bitter silence settled over ruined streets that only days before had known such exultant hopes. Nagy and those close to him were shipped out of Hungary and eventually executed by the Russians, who announced their deaths to an angry world in June 1958.

There have been few more melancholy chapters in recent human history, and the brutality of the Kremlin has left an enduring stain on the record of the Russian nation. Nor did the bloody episode add much to American prestige. Although the revolution made Soviet brutality plain for all the world to see, there is little doubt that American propaganda about "liberation" and "rolling back the Iron Curtain" encouraged many Hungarians to expect help that never came. The revolution would probably have broken out anyway, but many Americans have wondered whether the broadcasts of Radio Free Europe (a CIA operation) and the Voice of America (U.S. government radio) bore any responsibility for the tragic events of that incredible autumn.

It seems likely that no matter what its rhetoric, there was no way that the United States could have intervened directly to save the Hungarian people. The risks of direct action in an area where the Russians had every strategic and tactical advantage were too great. But perhaps the United States, and the West generally, could have taken some diplomatic or political action to lessen the suffering of the Hungarian people.

However, the West's hands were tied by the other great event of that 1956 autumn, the invasion of Suez by Israel with the military backing of Britain and France. These two nations, in what was their last attempt to act as the colonial masters of old, decided to take back the Suez Canal and topple the government of that nuisance, Nasser. Israel was glad to cooperate, hoping perhaps to end once and for all the Egyptian threat to its existence.

On October 29, while Hungary was in the early throes of its agony, Israeli columns struck into Egypt across the Sinai peninsula, and the next day French and British planes bombed Nasser's forces. This one-two punch would have soon defeated the Egyptians had it not been for the intervention of the United States and, to a lesser degree, of the United Nations and Russia.

Eisenhower was genuinely distressed by the attack on Egypt. He and Dulles simply believed it was wrong. The United States put heavy political and economic pressure on the British and French who, no longer the great powers they once were, lost their nerve. Although it was primarily the Americans who stopped the Suez invasion just hours before it would have succeeded, the Russians gained much of the credit, at least in the Arab world. Once they learned that the United States would not back its allies, they proclaimed to the world that the invasion had to stop or the invaders would face Soviet wrath. The Russians then commenced to rattle their atomic swords mightily, knowing they would not have to use them.

The Suez incident conclusively demonstrated to any doubters that the United States was now more powerful in the Middle East than the old imperialists, Britain and France. More important perhaps, it distracted attention from Russia's brutality in Hungary. No one can know, of course, but if the Suez crisis had not developed at the turning point of the Hungarian revolution, Khrushchev might have been more cautious in his actions. And even if Khrushchev had followed exactly the same course, with no Suez crisis to diffuse the moral considerations, the reactions of the West might well have been different. It was a bit difficult for the West to point the finger at the Kremlin when two of the three most important Western nations were attempting a blatant intervention in Egypt.

It was with this background that the American people went to the polls in 1956. During the campaign Adlai Stevenson had been attacked bitterly by then Vice President Nixon for suggesting that the United States seek an end to the testing of nuclear weapons. Nixon argued that a halt in testing nuclear weapons would play into the hands of the Communists. But Stevenson, a great humanist, had been profoundly influenced by the world-wide outcry against the hydrogen tests that had been regularly conducted by the United States since it developed the H-bomb in late 1952, and by the Soviet Union since 1953. Scientific tests had demonstrated to the horror of millions that radioactive fallout from the tests was contaminating the air, the seas, and even the food people ate. Ban the Bomb movements had sprung up all over the world, including the United States, and Stevenson became the spokesman for those who had become angry and frightened by the degree to which the two superpowers were blithely polluting man's total environment.

In November, though—even after events in Suez and Hungary had presumably demonstrated in the most tragic way the failure of Eisenhower's foreign policy—the electorate turned to the General more overwhelmingly than before, swamping Stevenson in a landslide.

10
Eisenhower's Final Term

ALTHOUGH 1956 had severely tested the established order on both sides of the Iron Curtain, and the passions aroused by Hungary and Suez were slow to cool, a gradual easing of tensions developed in 1957.

In a most ironic way, Hungary was somewhat responsible. Khrushchev had learned that despite its rhetoric, the United States would not intervene in the Russian sphere, for if it would not intervene under such extreme provocation, clearly it would never intervene. Thus, Russian fears of the United States abated somewhat and this encouraged Khrushchev in his campaign of peaceful competition.

This is not to say, however, that the unpredictable Khrushchev had become a passionate advocate of liberalism at home, as an incident described by LaFeber proves: "At a garden party, Khrushchev made such a verbal assault upon the invited intellectuals that one woman fainted. That harangue climaxed with Khrushchev shouting that Hungary would have remained orderly if several writers had been shot at the proper time; if such a threat ever faced the Soviet Union, he added, 'My hand would not tremble.' " [1]

But if America's reaction to Hungary had reassured Khrushchev, Russia's reaction had alarmed Eisenhower and Dulles. Thus, in January Eisenhower proposed to Congress what has come to be known as the Eisenhower Doctrine which, in effect, for a while at least, tried to extend the Monroe Doctrine to the Middle East. Fearing that a power vacuum had developed there after Suez, Dulles believed it necessary that the United States fill the vacuum before Russia could. The Eisenhower resolution proposed that the United States give military and economic aid to those Middle Eastern nations that requested it and called for American military aid "to secure and protect the territorial integrity and political independence of such nations, requesting such aid, against overt armed aggression from any nation controlled by International Communism."

This gave Eisenhower a free hand, an opportunity he soon took advantage of when the young, pro-Western King Hussein of Jordan asked for help against pro-Nasser elements within his country. Eisenhower dispatched the Sixth Fleet to the area and sent $10 million. In explaining the move, the State Department did not mention the "International Communism" aspect of the Doctrine. The action was to safeguard "the preservation of the independence and integrity of the nations of the Middle East." This was a prelude to the direct intervention in Lebanon a year later.

Around this time there began to emerge in the United States a questioning attitude toward America's posture in the Cold War. Although the people as a whole and most of the government clearly supported a hard line, there were those who thought the time was ripe for a disengagement in Europe between East and West. Prominent among them was George Kennan, one of the creators of the containment policy of a decade before.

Kennan proposed that before Germany received nuclear arms, "the threat of that possibility could be used to negotiate with the Russians a neutralization of Central and Eastern Europe which would include withdrawal of Soviet troops from the satellite countries." [2] The response to this from Dean Acheson was brusque. The former Secretary of State, no less a hard-liner than Dulles himself, asserted that if the United States under such an agreement withdrew its troops from Western Europe, Russia would sooner or later extinguish "independent national life in Western Europe." Yet before long even Dulles would begin to think that perhaps the time had come to modify American policies in light of changed circumstances.

Also in mid-1957 Khrushchev finally triumphed over the hard-liners in Moscow, and such famous and once-powerful Communists as Molotov, Malenkov, and Kaganovich were shunted off to lesser posts. Times had changed, however; they were merely demoted, not liquidated as in Stalin's day. And Khrushchev began to take the initiative in eye-catching disarmament proposals, largely for propaganda purposes, because neither side was yet ready to tackle the age-old question of whether disarmament comes before peace or peace before disarmament.

Russia always called for the withdrawal of troops from Central Europe and the removal of all foreign military bases. This sounded plausible enough, except that even if Russia withdrew all her troops, they were still within striking distance of the rest of Europe, whereas if the United States withdrew its forces, they were an ocean away. However, Khrushchev did make one proposal that soon he acted on unilaterally. He took a page from Adlai Stevenson's book and called for a moratorium on nuclear testing.

1957 also introduced a new word into the English vocabulary, a word which signaled the beginning of an exciting epoch in man's history: Sputnik. The space age began on the morning of October 4 when powerful Soviet booster rockets thrust "Travelling Companion" into orbit around the earth. Not only was it an astounding scientific and technological feat, but it had been accomplished by a nation considered far inferior to the United States in just those fields. And, more ominous, it meant that Russia would soon be able to fire the world's first intercontinental ballistic missiles.

Even though the United States was not far behind, the country suddenly experienced an overwhelming national inferiority complex. Almost overnight a series of crash programs in all areas were begun, including scientific and mathematical education right down to the kindergarten level. Needless to say, the enthusiasm for these crash programs soon began to fade.

As the year 1958 began, the world had changed. The Russians had sent Sputnik hurtling through space, and on January 31 the United States launched its Explorer I.

Other changes were less dramatic, more gradual. Thirty years before, Russia had been an almost primitive nation, huddled in suspicion behind poorly defended frontiers. And the United States had been an isolationist state with few political interests outside the Western hemisphere. Now Russia was the most powerful country in Europe, and the great historic nations of Britain, France, and Germany were no match for it. The United States, for its part, had men and bases girdling the globe. Centuries of domination by the nations of Western Europe were over; their glorious days of empire had ended. Two young and crude nations (many Europeans thought) now dominated the world.

Even their days of domination were numbered, however. Russia's problems with its empire had already been demonstrated in Hungary and, hidden to the rest of the world, its troubles with China were growing. In the West, America's allies were regaining their strength and on June 1, 1958 six European nations formed an economic union that would soon rival the United States in economic strength. (The birth of the Common Market provided further proof of the superiority of nationalism over Soviet-directed Communism, for both the Italian and Belgian Communists supported the Market despite Moscow's hostility.) Another step in European independence also came that same month when General Charles de Gaulle returned to power in France. To the dismay of many Americans, he was determined that France, and indeed all Western Europe, should not be subservient to the United States, and he often followed policies that have been termed anti-American.

A curious episode in American foreign policy began in July 1958. On the 14th a coup led by the pro-Nasser General Abdel Karim Kassim overthrew the monarchy in Iraq. That afternoon Eisenhower ordered 14,000 troops into nearby Lebanon, where a crisis had been developing for months, ever since the United States had proclaimed the Eisenhower Doctrine.

Virtually all the countries of the Middle East, including the pro-Western Jordan and Saudi Arabia, had spurned the American plan. Only Lebanon had accepted. President Camille Chamoun wanted American help to preserve his power and that of his party. He represented the Christian Arabs who ruled in a sometimes uneasy coalition with Muslim Arabs. Many of the Muslims became, after Suez, pan-Arab partisans of Nasser. This alarmed both Chamoun and the United States, but then his American support itself became a political issue. The situation continued to worsen and by mid-1958 there was virtual civil war.[3]

With the Kassim coup Washington decided it was time to intervene to preserve stability; Dulles spoke to Congressional leaders vaguely about "recent Soviet political activities" in the area and said "it was time to bring a halt to the deterioration in our position in the Middle East." A number of Congressmen said they had seen little or no evidence of Communist activity in Lebanon—and indeed there was none of any significance—and suggested that Dulles wanted the United States to intervene in Lebanese politics. However, they made no attempt to block Eisenhower's action. Thus, while British paratroopers landed in Jordan to support King Hussein, American troops waded ashore in Lebanon. It was quite a scene. Curious bathers lined the shores to watch the combat-ready troops hit the beaches and vendors tried to peddle their wares to soldiers carrying rifles at the ready.

When the Americans got to the Presidential Palace, they found Chamoun a virtual prisoner and totally out of touch with the situation. General Fuad Chehab, commander of the army, seemed to be the only one capable of dealing with the situation—he had espoused compromise all along—so the

United States abandoned Chamoun and allowed various factions to settle on Chehab, who was soon elected by Parliament to succeed Chamoun. The fighting died down and on October 25 the last of the U.S. marines sailed away from the beautiful city of Beirut. In the meantime General Kassim of Iraq had convinced the West that their interests were safe, although some months later, in March 1959, he withdrew Baghdad from the Baghdad Pact.

Thus it was that the American political intervention led to the internal turmoil that caused the American military intervention that helped quiet the internal turmoil. And as William G. Carleton has so aptly put it:

Within two years the United States dissipated much of the Arab and neutralist good will it had won during the Suez crisis. By attempting in its Eisenhower Doctrine to induce the neutral Arab states to become military allies, the United States precipitated events which merged Syria and Egypt into the United Arab Republic, converted Lebanon from an ally into a neutral, transformed Iraq from a Western military ally into a neutral with a distinct anti-Western flavor, immobilized King Saud, and isolated Jordan.[4]

Then on November 10 Khrushchev made a statement on Berlin that the West termed an ultimatum. Alarmed perhaps by the growing strength of West Germany—now much stronger militarily than East Germany—Khrushchev demanded that the Western troops pull their 10,000 troops out of West Berlin, agree to make Berlin a "free city" outside either power bloc (although being isolated in East Germany would no doubt influence its future course), and negotiate with East Germany, which the West did not recognize, for continued access to Berlin. And Khrushchev insisted that if there were no agreement within six months, he would turn the allied access routes over to East German jurisdiction. Dulles interpreted this as another full-scale Berlin crisis and responded firmly. But the crisis never came to much. In February 1959 Khrushchev told British Prime Minister Harold Macmillan on a Moscow visit not to take the time limit too seriously, and during Big Four foreign ministers' meetings in the spring and summer Soviet Foreign Minister Andrei Gromyko said negotiations could take a year or so.

1959 saw continued relaxation in the tensions of the Cold War, although it began with an event that was later to strain Russian-American relations and even, for a few anxious days, world peace.

On January 1 a triumphant Fidel Castro, his brother Raul and Ernesto "Che" Guevara at his side, marched into Havana. His years of rebellion were over. The Batista regime had collapsed, more as a result of its own corruption and incompetence than of the daring guerrilla warfare carried on from the Sierra Maestra by the Fidelistas. But although of great interest to Americans—Cuba had long been an adjunct to the American economy and it was a favorite resort—it didn't seem all that important at the time, just another Latin nation changing rulers.

In May, John Foster Dulles died, after having resigned in April. Few men have had as great impact on American foreign policy as he. A man of great stature, conviction, and drive, he nevertheless brought to foreign affairs a puritanical, moralistic philosophy that almost inevitably meant a rigid policy. Perhaps he would have subscribed to this statement by John Spanier:

If the United States is by definition moral, it obviously cannot compromise; for a nation endowed with a moral mission can hardly violate its own principles. That would constitute appeasement and national humiliation. The nation's principles would be transgressed, the nation's interests improperly defended, the national honor stained. For to compromise with the immoral enemy is to be contaminated with evil. Moreover, to reach a settlement with him, rather than wiping him out in order to safeguard our principles, would be a recognition of our weakness.[5]

Many critics have suggested that this moralistic streak in the American character is responsible for many of our foreign policy failures. Not that it is wrong for a nation to hold moral considerations high—as, to its credit, the United States often has—but to believe that the American view is the only possible one, that only it recognizes morality, can lead this nation —and others—to believe that what it does is right simply because it does it.

Even Dulles in the last months of his life recognized that circumstances had changed over a decade. "He no longer feared that the Soviets would pose a greater threat with their disavowal of force and 'this policy of the smile,' " LaFeber relates. "Dulles found hope in the belief 'that a nation tends to become what it pretends to be. . . . I have seen lots of tough guys who have made their pile, who come to New York, wanted to get into society, and who have to behave differently.' The Secretary of State attempted to readjust American military thinking by placing increased emphasis on small nuclear weapons which could be used in limited wars." [6]

Even with his changing view of the Cold War, Dulles might have been shocked by the extraordinary visit of Nikita Khrushchev to America that September. The stocky, unpredictable Khrushchev crisscrossed America, a volatile bundle of amiability who tossed ears of corn at American newsmen and pouted because the Secret Service for security reasons wouldn't let him see Disneyland. Despite the enormous publicity, it is hard to say exactly what the trip accomplished. At its end Khrushchev and Eisenhower met privately at the President's retreat outside Washington, Camp David, but nothing specific came of it, except a return invitation for Eisenhower to visit Russia the following year and a somewhat improved atmosphere that was termed by the Russian press as "the Spirit of Camp David," much as it had referred to "the Spirit of Geneva" four years before.

On the way back from the United States, Khrushchev stopped off in Peking to reassure Mao that no Russian-American deals had been made at China's expense. This was then, and has continued to be, a major Chinese concern. Indeed, it is a concern of all three powers: the United States, Russia, and China are each forever worried that the other two might combine against it.

Eisenhower's visit to Russia in 1960 would no doubt have had tremendous impact. Not only was the President of the United States the most important figure in the world, but Eisenhower was also remembered in Russia as a great hero of the war against Hitler. But the visit was never to take place.

On May 1, two weeks before Eisenhower was to meet Khrushchev, Macmillan, and de Gaulle in Paris, the Russians shot down an American U-2 plane deep inside Russia. The United States immediately said it was a weather plane on a research mission in the Middle East and that if it had entered Russia, the intrusion was accidental. The incident simmered for a couple of days and then Khrushchev himself announced that the plane had been recovered and that the pilot, who had been captured alive, had signed a confession that he had been on a spy mission.

This electrified the world. The United States had, of course, little choice but to admit that it had been caught red-handed both in spying and in lying about it. And then, in an extraordinary turnabout, the United States admitted that U-2 flights had been going on for several years.

William G. Carleton describes the aftermath:

Neutral and even Allied opinion was shocked by these activities of the United States, which were contrary to international law and certainly extraordinary in actual practice. Even many Americans who agreed that such flights were prudent safeguards against surprise attack were exasperated that such flights had been allowed to continue in the weeks prior to the summit conference. Khrushchev gave the President an "out" by declaring that he did not believe the President himself could have known of such flights, but the President cut the ground from under him by taking personal responsibility for the flights, though it appeared that he had not authorized this particular one. Moreover, the President justified these flights (and thus intimated that they would be continued) by saying that distasteful as such intelligence-gathering activities might be, the safety of the free world made them indispensable.[7]

There was considerable hypocrisy in the condemnation of the United States, for in the modern world spying of all sorts is done by many nations as a matter of course. Where the United States was open to particular criticism was in the clumsiness with which the whole situation was handled and the way that Eisenhower at first implied that the spy missions would continue (although at Paris later he said the over-flights would not continue) even though the whole world knew about them. But Russia must have been embarrassed too, not only in the eyes of the world but of its own people. How was it possible that American planes for years had been penetrating Russian air space without being shot down? How much had the United States learned about Russian defenses?

Thus, it was not surprising that Khrushchev took the offensive when the summit meeting opened in Paris in mid-May. What was surprising was the offensive way in which he took the offensive, screaming like a fishwife and demanding that Eisenhower apologize publicly. Eisenhower, who must have been terribly uncomfortable, conducted himself with dignity and declined to apologize under such circumstances. So the summit talks collapsed, and with them Eisenhower's visit to Russia.

One can only speculate about Khrushchev's motives for his rude behavior. Was he really that distressed over the U-2 flights, was he attempting to score a propaganda victory, or had he changed his mind about the desirability of a summit meeting? But however tough Khrushchev was at Paris, he still pushed for peaceful coexistence, he still was prepared to wait a while longer on Berlin, and he publicly hoped for another summit meeting when Eisenhower's successor had taken office. And if Khrushchev was tough on Eisenhower, he was even tougher on Mao during a meeting of the Rumanian Communist party in Bucharest in June. The schism between the giant Communist neighbors was getting increasingly hard to paper over; the natural rivalry was triumphing over Communist unity.

By the fall of 1960, while John F. Kennedy and Richard M.

Nixon were contesting for the right to succeed Eisenhower, events had taken place in Indochina that would greatly influence the Presidency of first Kennedy and then, eight years later, of Nixon.

Ever since 1955 Ho Chi Minh had been seeking the all-Vietnam elections promised by the 1954 Geneva Agreements. But the Diem regime in South Vietnam, with the complete backing of the United States, refused to abide by the agreement. Ho's followers in the south grew more and more impatient, but he counseled more patience while he built up the economy of North Vietnam and continued to work politically for the reunification of the country. As Diem's repression in the south continued to grow, however, Ho was no longer able to restrain the Vietminh in the south. Late in 1960, the National Liberation Front was formed (the guerrilla arm of which has since gained fame as the Viet Cong) and was recognized shortly thereafter by Ho's regime in the north.

The storm was gathering.

11

The Kennedy Years

JOHN F. KENNEDY won the 1960 election primarily on his personal appeal, for there was not a great deal of difference between his program and that advanced by Vice President Nixon. Both were young men but Kennedy was handsome, poised, and witty, a splendid television performer, and he took the offensive throughout, promising that he "would get the country moving again." He won by only a little over a hundred thousand votes, overcoming in the process the handicap of being a Roman Catholic, the first ever to win the Presidency.

Even before Kennedy could take office on January 20, 1961, his role in the Cold War was being partially prescribed for him. On January 3 the outgoing Eisenhower Administration broke diplomatic relations with Cuba, an act that might better have been left for the new Administration. There had been growing hostility between Fidel Castro and Washington since shortly after he took power in Havana on the first day of 1959. His revolution was not like the many earlier ones in

Cuba and elsewhere in Latin America; Castro meant to make real changes.

There was no way that revolutionary changes could be reconciled with the almost total American domination of the Cuban economy. Castro wanted to end this domination and he took steps to do so by nationalizing some American industries. This inevitably antagonized the giant corporations, and with them the American government.

Along with this growing tension there began to be charges that Castro was a Communist and had been one all along. Eventually he did proclaim himself a Communist and there were those in the United States who said: "I told you so." But others argued that Castro had become a Communist because the Cuban Communist party was the only organized group that he could call upon to help govern the island nation, a task that became increasingly difficult as the United States retaliated against nationalization by cutting American exports to Cuba. In any case, there is no real evidence that Castro was a Communist before his triumph, and considerable evidence that the Communists opposed his revolution because he was too independent.

Wanting to diminish Cuban reliance on the sale of sugar to the United States, Castro began selling it to Russia and China. This further angered the United States and on July 7, 1960 President Eisenhower eliminated the Cuban sugar quota for the rest of the year. This was a step that once would have been considered fatal to the Cuban economy, but it managed to limp along, turning partly of necessity and partly of choice to Communist nations for trade and aid.

As the sides exchanged charges and countercharges, Cuba on the last day of 1960 asked for an urgent meeting of the

United Nations Security Council, accusing the United States
of preparing an imminent invasion of Cuba. The United
States denied the charges, as it did new accusations of establishing training bases in Honduras, Guatemala, and Florida
for such an invasion, and it was then that Eisenhower broke
diplomatic relations. The Cubans evidently hoped for better
relations under Kennedy, for on January 5 they blamed the
rupture on Eisenhower.

While that situation simmered, Eisenhower made a fare-
well address, one that many consider the most important
speech of his career. On January 17 he said:

We have been compelled to create a permanent armaments industry of vast proportions. Added to this, three and a half million
men and women are directly engaged in the defense establishment. We annually spend on military security alone more than
the net income of all United States corporations.

Now this conjunction of an immense military establishment
and a large arms industry is new in the American experience. The
total influence—economic, political, even spiritual—is felt in
every city, every state house, every office of the Federal Government. We recognize the imperative need for this development.
Yet we must not fail to comprehend its grave implications. Our
toil, resources and livelihood are all involved; so is the very
structure of our society.

In the councils of government, we must guard against the
acquisition of unwarranted influence, whether sought or un-
sought, by the military-industrial complex. The potential for
disastrous rise of misplaced power exists and will persist.

We must never let the weight of this combination endanger
our liberties or democratic processes. We should take nothing for
granted. Only an alert and knowledgeable citizenry can compel

the proper meshing of the huge industrial and military machinery of defense with our peaceful methods and goals, so that security and liberty may prosper together.[1]

But although this extraordinary statement by a man who had been a military man all his adult life has been quoted innumerable times, it has had little if any effect on subsequent Presidents, for the defense budget has continued to grow and with it the inevitable influence of the "military-industrial complex."

Three days later John Fitzgerald Kennedy took office and in his eloquent inaugural address said: "Let us never negotiate out of fear but let us never fear to negotiate." Those Americans who thought the Cold War had gone on too long, that it was diverting American resources and energy from pressing domestic problems, were encouraged. Here was a young man with fresh attitudes who would lead America away from the rigid policies of the Eisenhower-Dulles years.

This was an illusion; for from the first days of the Kennedy Administration stories began to circulate that the United States, despite its denials in the UN, was preparing an invasion of Cuba by exiles. The *New York Times* had almost the whole story on April 7 but in response to pressure from the White House eliminated the most significant details.

On April 17, 1400 brave Cuban exiles, recruited, trained, equipped, financed, and transported by the United States, hit the beaches on the then unknown Bay of Pigs. It was a disaster in every possible way: military, political, psychological, even moral—perhaps especially moral. The military operations were bungled, the cover story was transparent, Castro's armed forces performed well contrary to American expectation, and there was not even a hint of the general uprising that the CIA had assured Kennedy would follow the landing.

The CIA and the Pentagon—both civilian and military— had bungled incredibly; not one of Kennedy's senior advisers had counseled against the landing; other top aides who might have been expected to oppose it were not notified or were told too late; and, most important, Kennedy himself had given the go-ahead to this adventure. Despite the fact that the planning had begun during the Eisenhower Administration, the responsibility was entirely Kennedy's.[2]

Again, the basic question: Does one nation ever have the right to intervene directly in the domestic affairs of another and if so, under what circumstances? Together with that: Has the United States in recent decades understood the widespread demand for change in the world, and has it been able to distinguish when revolutions are indigenous, whether Communist or not, and when they have been directed and controlled by Moscow or Peking?

Within a couple of days the abortive invasion had collapsed, most of the invaders had been killed or captured, and the entire world, not just Communist and neutralist nations, was in an uproar. A badly shaken Kennedy publicly accepted the blame but he was not one to sulk over past blunders. He went ahead constructing his foreign policy, a key element of which was, particularly after the Bay of Pigs, the Alliance for Progress, a mammoth economic aid program for Latin America. But this project was plagued with difficulties from the beginning. There were bureaucratic difficulties in Washington; some of the most important Latin American countries would not allow their development plans to be closely examined; and, most significant, few of the recipient countries would make the political, economic, and social changes on which the success of the Alliance depended.

In May, Kennedy sent his Vice President, former Senate Majority Leader Lyndon B. Johnson, to Vietnam. Foreshadowing the decision he would make as President, Johnson called South Vietnam's President Diem "the Winston Churchill of Asia" and warned Kennedy that the United States had to make a "fundamental decision . . . whether to attempt to meet the challenge of Communist expansion now in Southeast Asia . . . or throw in the towel." [3] In October, Kennedy sent his friend and trusted adviser, General Maxwell Taylor, to Vietnam along with another top adviser, Walt W. Rostow, an advocate of "counter-insurgency," a term meaning fighting guerrillas with their own techniques that became very popular in Washington during the Kennedy years. They, too, advocated complete support for the authoritarian Diem and called for increasing U.S. military aid.

Important as it was, though, Vietnam was never a primary concern of Kennedy's. Even more pressing matters occupied his attention. In June he met Khrushchev. Each was eager to take the measure of the other. It was an eye-opener for Kennedy, for Khrushchev was tough in their Vienna meeting, thinking perhaps that Kennedy would be on the defensive after the Bay of Pigs. Although they reached agreement on the three-sided civil war in Laos, Khrushchev insisted that an understanding be reached soon on the infinitely more important Germany—after all, the war had been over for sixteen years and there was still no peace treaty. He said he was going to make peace with East Germany soon, with or without the West.

Khrushchev also spoke about Russia's right to help in "wars of national liberation." This, too, alarmed Kennedy, although it was already quite evident that where Communist governments were established by local revolutionaries independent of the Red Army—as in China, Albania, and Yugoslavia—national interests dominated, often to the point of alienating them from Moscow.

In this respect, Kennedy and his advisers were like the Eisenhower Administration; they interpreted any revolution with any degree of Communist participation, even if purely local, as a threat to American security. Many critics of American foreign policy have argued that this becomes a threat only when America intervenes and thus involves American security. However, when there was no element of Communism, as in Africa generally, Kennedy applauded, even assisted, self-determination. Cool and sophisticated as he was, he had been conditioned, as had most Americans, by a decade and a half of anti-Communist rhetoric.

Shortly after returning from Vienna, Kennedy, on July 25, called reserve troops to duty and announced an increase of nearly 25 per cent in American military strength. Kennedy had evidently accepted the judgment of Dean Acheson that the Berlin issue was a "simple conflict of wills." He wanted Khrushchev to know that an American President could not be browbeaten. In his dramatic national broadcast announcing the military buildup, Kennedy declared that the Berlin "outpost is not an isolated problem. The threat is world-wide. . . ." This sober talk aroused great fear in the United States and for a while there was something of a war scare, with bomb shelters suddenly becoming fashionable, a trend that was exploited immediately by the imaginative entrepreneurs of this new industry that sprang up overnight.

Now it was Khrushchev's move and he made one that horrified the world. On August 13, without warning, the Russians and East Germans began constructing a concrete wall topped with barbed wire all along the border between East and West Berlin. This was an admission of failure, for thousands of East Germans, often that regime's most valuable people, young professionals and technicians, had fled to the West by the simple expedient of crossing from East Berlin to West and asking for asylum. They would then be flown out of Berlin to West Germany. East Germans continued to try to escape to the West, but the Wall made it much harder and many were killed. The United States and West Germany protested the Wall, and people all over the world, government leaders and individuals, expressed shock. But the Wall stood, a physical symbol of a divided Germany and a divided world.

Khrushchev had more to come. On August 31 he announced that the Soviet Union would end its self-imposed three-year moratorium on nuclear testing with the largest blast ever exploded. (The United States and Great Britain had followed Russia's example and also stopped testing.) The UN General Assembly almost unanimously appealed to Russia not to resume testing, but Khrushchev ignored world opinion and began a series of tests climaxed with one in November of more than fifty megatons, more than 3000 times more powerful than the weapons the United States had used to destroy Hiroshima and Nagasaki. Perhaps Khrushchev was trying to show Kennedy that he, too, was tough or perhaps he was trying to overcome the effect of the newly announced information by the American Defense Depart-

ment that Russia had only a "handful" of operational intercontinental ballistic missiles.

A few days after Khrushchev's announcement, Kennedy
announced that the United States would resume underground testing, taking great care that the atmosphere not be
polluted. Some top advisers tried to convince him that the
U.S. nuclear lead was such that he did not have to resume
testing at all, that by holding off, the United States would
score a huge propaganda victory. That may have been so, but
on March 2 of the next year, Kennedy, convinced of its
military necessity, announced that the United States would
also resume atmospheric tests.

1962 was John Kennedy's only full year in office and he
began it by sending two air-support companies of 300 men
to Saigon, "the first of a steady succession of small increments
that would bring the level up to about 25,000 by the summer
of 1964. The President had rejected major military intervention as a conscious policy but he had set in force the
bureaucratic momentum that would make it a certainty." [4]
Kennedy had long been critical of French colonial rule in
Indochina and he realized that sending in troops usually led
to sending in more troops. "It's like taking a drink," he once
remarked. "The effect wears off and you have to take
another." Also he was dubious about Eisenhower's domino
theory, but he had been convinced by his advisers that all
Southeast Asia was at stake. So he began what was clearly
meant to be a small-scale intervention of limited duration.

What Kennedy feared might happen indeed began to
happen. The more Diem needed American support to stay
in power, the more arrogant he became. As the American
commitment increased, he became convinced that the United

States had no alternative but to support him. And for years, until finally he went too far in his increasingly dictatorial rule, he was right; there was an increasing interdependence between Diem and the Americans.

Even as Kennedy was raising military expenditures, in response to what he regarded as Russian aggressiveness, a panel of economists reported to the U.S. Arms Control and Disarmament Agency that about $120 billion were spent annually on military budgets by the nations of the world. This amounted to about two thirds of the total annual income of the developing countries. The economists said that if only a "fraction" of that were diverted to the needy nations, it would result in a marked increase in the rate of growth of real income in the poorer parts of the world. But such a diversion was not to be; the American military expenditures would continue to rise for years to come and foreign aid would decrease.

Perhaps Kennedy did not have time to consider this report, for it was not long before he was engaged in another crisis, this time in Laos. Here there were three main factions, right-wing, neutralist, and pro-Communist, all engaged in constant struggle. In 1957 the neutralists were in control, but in 1958 the leftists won substantial victories in the elections. The neutralist Premier, Prince Souvanna Phouma, resigned and a right-wing group took over the government, receiving U.S. support. But Russia, China, and the Vietminh helped the Communist Pathet Lao forces against the right-wing government which then, of course, received even more U.S. aid.

Early in 1960 the right wing won the elections but later that year neutralist and leftist (albeit avowedly non-Communist) elements in the army overthrew the right-wing government and the neutralist, Prince Souvanna Phouma, returned to rule. Then there were rival right-wing and neutralist governments, with the United States giving aid to both. Again the neutralist prince resigned, the rightists occupied the capital of Vientiane and the civil war grew more intense, with the Communist Pathet Lao gaining in strength. As chances for a direct Russian-American confrontation grew in 1961, Britain convinced both sides to negotiate.

The negotiations dragged on from May 1961 to June 1962 when agreement was reached that Laos would remain neutral. Although there has been frequent fighting and continued confusion, with the Pathet Lao reportedly gaining strength, the fragile neutrality agreement has lasted until this writing. The results have been far from satisfactory to either side, but much better than a situation that could have led to direct intervention by either Russia or the United States or China or all three.[5]

The neutralization of neighboring Laos encouraged the National Liberation Front in South Vietnam to seek the same goal. On July 20, 1962, the eighth anniversary of the signing of the Geneva Agreements, the NLF proposed a four-point program: 1. the withdrawal of U.S. troops; 2. a cessation of hostilities through "a settlement of internal affairs by the South Vietnamese themselves"; 3. a coalition government representing all groups in South Vietnam; and 4. ". . . A badly-needed international agreement . . . to enable the powers from different camps to guarantee respect for the sovereignty, independence, territorial integrity and neutrality of South Viet Nam which is ready to form a neutral zone together with Cambodia and Laos, three States enjoying full sovereign rights."

Observers of the situation in Southeast Asia have often said that any eventual agreement would require a coalition government in Vietnam and the establishment of the area as an internationally-guaranteed neutral zone. These very points were made by the NLF before American escalation began. Further, and this is significant, the NLF spoke of South Vietnam as "sovereign," hardly a welcome term to its brothers in North Vietnam. Whereas the U.S. government has always claimed that the NLF and its Viet Cong were controlled by the North, the NLF itself has always made a point of its distinctiveness. And the NLF has long said that South Vietnam would be reunited with the North only after negotiations and the passage of time. Thus, many critics have made the point that the American intervention, particularly after the large-scale intervention began, has driven the South Vietnamese rebels closer to the North through military necessity. In any case, Diem, with United States backing, rejected the NLF proposals and the course of the civil war became even more bitter.

It must be remembered, however, that Southeast Asia in those days was a matter of low priority in the Kennedy Administration. Not only did the young President have to cope with domestic problems but the United States was engaged in a major effort in the Congo, leading the United Nations effort to restore stability to that strife-torn infant nation. Then there were the perennial questions of Berlin, relations with Russia, disarmament and nuclear testing, the frustrating Alliance for Progress, and again, Cuba.

In September 1962, American concern once more began to grow over the island. Russia had been arming Cuba—which feared another attack from the United States, direct or indirect—and on September 4 Kennedy warned sternly that although there was "no evidence" of "significant offensive capability" in Cuban hands, "were it otherwise, the gravest issues would arise." A few days later Khrushchev replied that the "armaments and military equipment sent to Cuba are designed exclusively for defensive purposes. There is no need for the Soviet Union to shift its weapons for the repulsion of aggression, for a retaliatory blow, to any other country, for instance Cuba. Our nuclear weapons are so powerful in their explosive force and the Soviet Union has such powerful rockets to carry these nuclear warheads that there is no need to search for sites for them beyond the boundaries of the Soviet Union." [6]

On September 13 at a press conference Kennedy said the Soviet shipments were not yet a serious threat; however, he was blunt in his warning to Russia and Cuba that if the island were to "become an offensive military base of significant capacity for the Soviet Union, then this country will do whatever must be done to protect its own security and that of its allies." He also doubled the number of U-2 flights over Cuba. At first, they observed nothing of significance but then on October 14 a plane returned with photographs of a launching pad, a number of associated buildings, and even a missile lying on the ground. Immediately Kennedy convened a series of top-level meetings to consider the appropriate action. Initially the feeling was for air strikes to knock out the missile sites before they could become operational. But opinion shifted against this. Some, like his brother and closest confidant, Attorney General Robert F. Kennedy, thought it was simply wrong for a great nation suddenly to attack a smaller. Others feared such an attack might trigger a nuclear response from Russia.[7]

The President finally decided on a naval blockade, or "quarantine," as it was called for public-relations purposes. He announced the existence of the Soviet missile sites to a stunned nationwide radio and television audience at 7 P.M., October 22. He told an anxious world—and Nikita Khrushchev—that "any nuclear missile launched from Cuba against any nation in the Western hemisphere" would be deemed "an attack by the Soviet Union on the United States, requiring a full retaliatory response upon the Soviet Union." And he called on Khrushchev to remove the missiles.

That was Monday night. Tuesday and Tuesday night dragged on with still no reply from Khrushchev and Russian ships were getting closer to the American blockade. There was widespread fear all over the world that the two great powers were on the verge of nuclear war, the dread of which had underlain all man's activities since Hiroshima.

A pall hung over the people of the United States. Many, fearing the worst, mobbed the supermarkets, buying any and all canned goods still on the shelves. And some, living in large urban centers certain to be prime targets in an all-out war, quietly left on unexpected vacations. Others simply waited helplessly. Radios and television sets were on all over the country as people eagerly sought reassurance that a nuclear holocaust was not to come.

On Wednesday, United Nations Secretary-General U Thant made a significant intervention. He suggested a cooling-off period by having Russia suspend arms shipments for two or three weeks while the United States did the same with its blockade. The next day, Thursday, Thant received a message from Khrushchev accepting the proposal. Thant's initiative had given the Russians a face-saving way to back away from confrontation. They could say they were responding to his initiative, not to Kennedy's ultimatum. That same day Thant heard from Kennedy, who kept the door open for discussion but still insisted that the missiles be removed.

Armed with these replies, Thant sent off more specific messages to the two leaders, asking Khrushchev that his ships not challenge the American blockade and asking Kennedy to avoid a direct confrontation with the Soviet ships. Because of faster communications between Washington and New York, Thant got Kennedy's response the same day. If Soviet ships stayed away from the interception zone, the President said, the United States would avoid a direct confrontation. On Friday, Thant received Khrushchev's reply; he had ordered his ships to stay away from the interception zone. With that, although the world did not yet know it, the worst was over. Even though there were still anxious moments as the United States and Russia worked out an agreement by which the Soviet Union would remove its missiles and the United States would pledge not to invade Cuba, it was just a matter of time.

The agreement was reached in a series of letters between Khrushchev and Kennedy, with Khrushchev saying that if the United States would promise not to invade Cuba or allow anyone else to, Russia would remove the missiles. Both leaders had been sobered by their approach to the brink of nuclear war, and Khrushchev also suggested that the two countries not only settle the Cuban crisis but attempt to ease all tensions between the two great powers. To this Kennedy replied:

The effect of such a settlement on easing world tensions would enable us to work toward a more general arrangement regarding "other armament," as proposed in your second letter, which you made public. I would like to say again that the United States is very much interested in reducing tensions and halting the arms race; and if your letter signifies that you are prepared to discuss a *détente* affecting NATO and the Warsaw Pact, we are quite prepared to consider with our allies any useful proposals.[8]

Thus, what had been the most frightening few days since the end of World War II developed into a period of genuine desire on both sides for an improvement in relations.

There have been many guesses—and they are only that—as to why Khrushchev took the gamble of installing Russian missiles in Cuba, but until such time, if ever, that the Kremlin records are available, we cannot know for sure. The most obvious reason—but one rejected by Washington—is that Khrushchev genuinely wanted to help Castro defend Cuba which, in view of the Bay of Pigs, did have a legitimate fear of the United States. It is also possible that Khrushchev wanted to use the missiles to lessen or overcome America's nuclear superiority, or he may have intended them for bargaining—perhaps for American concessions on Berlin or Germany as a whole; perhaps to use in bartering for the removal of American missile bases in Turkey and Italy.

Whatever the reason, it was a reckless move. Although Khrushchev had every legal right to put his missiles in Cuba with Castro's permission, just as the United States had the right to put missiles within range of Russia, it was nonetheless dangerous. Anyone with the slightest knowledge of the

United States, of its dedication to the Monroe Doctrine, should have realized that no President, regardless of the legalities, could allow such weapons so close to the United States. But reckless as Khrushchev was in making the attempt, he was prudent in his response once he realized Kennedy's determination. And although he did have to back down for all the world—including his colleagues in the Kremlin—to see, Khrushchev did gain what must have been one of his main goals: America's promise not to attack Cuba.

As for Vietnam, although the situation there continued to deteriorate in 1963, Kennedy paid it comparatively little attention; he was much more concerned with the aftermath of the Cuban missile crisis. On June 10 at the American University in Washington, Kennedy made what many have hailed as the finest speech of his life. He said peace was not possible unless the Soviet leaders adopted a new attitude. "I hope they do. I believe we can help them do it." Then Kennedy, who had less than six months to live, pronounced a sentence that could have meant he was planning a whole new direction for American foreign policy: "But I believe that we must re-examine our own attitude—as individuals and as a Nation—for our attitude is as essential as theirs." Many writers had long believed that such a re-examination was long overdue and if Kennedy had lived long enough to initiate it, it would have been one of the most significant Presidential actions in the second half of this century.

This speech, which Khrushchev later told Averell Harriman was the best by an American since Roosevelt, helped get off to a good start the negotiations in Moscow for a treaty to ban the testing of nuclear weapons. For several weeks that summer Russia, Britain, and the United States, its team headed by Harriman, negotiated and finally agreed on a treaty prohibiting nuclear test explosions in the atmosphere, outer space, and underwater. The Underground tests were not included because Russia would not agree to inspection within the Soviet Union, a manifestation of its longtime suspicion of outsiders. It argued that in the present state of science, no on-the-spot inspection was required. The United States, on the other hand, claimed that it was not always possible to distinguish between underground tests and earthquakes, so the two nations decided to eliminate that area from the ban, probably to the relief of the military on both sides.

Nonetheless, the treaty was a memorable event, for it meant that the United States, Russia, and Britain would no longer conduct the tests that had been polluting the earth and atmosphere since mid-1945. This was probably the greatest achievement of Kennedy's brief time in office, but it was also an achievement for Khrushchev, for the agreement of both leaders was essential.

There was another major shortcoming of the treaty besides the exclusion of underground tests. That was the refusal of both China and France to sign it. They have often been condemned for not doing so, but the blunt fact is that neither the United States nor Russia would have signed the treaty if they had not possessed an ample supply of nuclear weapons. There is simply not enough trust in the world for any great power to concede to other great powers, whether allies or not, such a staggering superiority in military strength.

The treaty was signed in Moscow on August 5, 1963. It was considered such an important occasion that United Nations Secretary-General U Thant journeyed to Russia for the signing. And accompanying Secretary of State Dean Rusk

was UN Ambassador Adlai Stevenson, who, as the Democratic nominee in 1956, had suggested such a ban on nuclear
testing, only to be attacked scornfully by then Vice President
Nixon. The treaty was ratified by the Senate (80 to 19) on
September 24.

With that ratification Kennedy could with confidence look
forward to other steps to solidify the *détente* developing between the United States and the Soviet Union. But events
which would postpone that cherished *détente* were moving
swiftly and soon would dominate the world stage.

In Vietnam, Ngo Dinh Diem had become more arrogant
than ever and had become engaged in what was almost a civil
war within a civil war with the majority Buddhists. The government was all but paralyzed and the fight against the Viet
Cong languished. With at least American consent, for it is
incredible that the huge American establishment in Saigon
under Ambassador Henry Cabot Lodge did not know of the
developments, an army coup overthrew Diem on November
1. Within hours he and his brother, head of the security
forces, were murdered. Arthur Schlesinger has written:

I saw the President soon after he heard that Diem and Nhu were
dead. He was somber and shaken. I had not seen him so depressed
since the Bay of Pigs. No doubt he realized that Vietnam was his
great failure in foreign policy, and that he had never really given
it his full attention. But the fact that the Vietnamese seemed
ready to fight had made him feel that there was a reasonable
chance of making a go of it. Yet, with his memory of the French
in Indochina in 1951, he had always believed there was a point at
which our intervention might turn Vietnamese nationalism
against us and transform an Asian civil conflict into a white man's
war. When he came into office, 2000 American troops were in

Vietnam. Now there were 16,000. How many more could there be before we passed the point? By 1961 choices had already been fatally narrowed; but still, if Vietnam had been handled as a political rather than a military problem, if . . . if, if, if—and now it was all past, and Diem miserably dead.[9]

There can be no doubt that Kennedy had decided that he must concentrate on Vietnam, but he himself was to live for only another three weeks. Whatever he might have done in Vietnam—withdrawn, escalated, sought a political solution either within Vietnam itself or by means of another international conference like that in Geneva in 1954—it was now too late. No one can ever know what he would have done; one can only speculate.

Whatever, the glamorous Kennedy years were ended violently on that November 22 in Dallas. He had served for only three years, years beset with enormous problems, but he had been confident that in the 1964 election he would receive a great mandate instead of the narrow victory of 1960 and that, equally important, he would sweep into office a liberal Congress that would give him the legislation denied by the sluggish, conservative Congresses of the past two sessions.

But his promise remained just that, for he was dead.

12

The Johnson Years

WHEN a somber Lyndon Baines Johnson succeeded to the leadership of a grieving nation in 1963, he assumed along with President Kennedy's powers his problems—and now foremost among them was Vietnam.

At this moment the new President could have chosen a new course but perhaps understandably he chose the one that had been charted by his predecessor, a cautious, gradual increase in American military strength.[1] Johnson kept on as his chief advisers those who had been instrumental in setting the present policy: Dean Rusk, Robert McNamara, McGeorge Bundy, and Walt Rostow. Such a policy was congenial to him for, as we saw, Johnson as Vice President had counseled a tough anti-Communist posture in Vietnam.

Thus, it was no surprise, considering the viewpoints of Johnson and his advisers, that the new President sent to Saigon this New Year's message:

Neutralization of South Vietnam would only be another name for a Communist takeover. . . . The United States will continue to furnish you and your people with the fullest measure of support in this bitter fight. . . . We shall maintain in Vietnam American personnel and matériel as needed to assist you in achieving victory.[2]

During his first months in office the Johnson Administration rejected publicly time and again overtures for another Geneva Conference. They came from UN Secretary-General U Thant and French President de Gaulle, as well as from Moscow, Hanoi, the National Liberation Front in South Vietnam, and, it must be emphasized, from Peking. There is simply no doubt that the United States could have had negotiations in 1964 merely by saying Yes. But as the Administration made clear, it did not want negotiations when Saigon was losing the war, when the Viet Cong held all the cards.

A turning point in the war came in August 1964. On August 2, according to the American announcement, North Vietnamese torpedo boats launched an "unprovoked" attack on the destroyer *Maddox* while it was on "routine patrol in international waters in the Gulf of Tonkin . . . about thirty miles at sea from the mainland of North Vietnam." The *Maddox* suffered no damage. Then on August 4 the United States said that North Vietnamese PT boats had attacked the *Maddox* and another destroyer, the *C. Turner Joy*, about sixty-five miles off the coast. Again, no damage. That night President Johnson went on nationwide radio and television to tell the American people that in response U.S. planes were carrying out attacks on three major naval bases in North Vietnam. The Pentagon later announced that all three bases were demolished, twenty-five boats were damaged or destroyed, and that the fuel depots were almost totally destroyed.

Even more important to the quickening pace of events was the action requested from Congress by President Johnson. He proposed—and got—a resolution supporting the President's "determination . . . to take all necessary measures to repel any armed attack against the forces of the United States and to prevent further aggression." It further said that the United States was "prepared, as the President determines, to take all necessary steps, including the use of armed force, to assist any member or protocol state of the Southeast Asian Collective Defense Treaty requesting assistance in defense of its freedom." On August 7, the resolution passed the House by 416 to 0 and the Senate by 98 to 2, with only Senators Wayne Morse and Ernest Greuning voting Nay. It was a demonstration of support neither Congress nor the American public would soon be allowed to forget, for the Johnson Administration would cite the Tonkin Resolution over and over again as the authority for the escalation of the war that followed.

There is still considerable confusion about the Tonkin incidents. In the first place, just before the August 2 incident, Hanoi accused the U.S. Navy of participating in the bombardment of some North Vietnamese islands. In the second, Rear Admiral Robert B. Moore was reported in the *New York Times* of August 11 as saying that the *Maddox* may have been in territorial waters claimed by North Vietnam. If either were true, the character of the incident was entirely different than reported. Further, Hanoi claimed that the second incident, the joint attack on the *Maddox* and the *C. Turner Joy*, had never taken place at all.

A number of Americans began to suspect that Washington had been less than candid, among them Senator William Fulbright, chairman of the Foreign Relations Committee. Political analyst Haynes Johnson describes the Arkansas Senator's reaction:

In the bitter aftermath, Fulbright believed he and the entire Congress had been deceived. The resolution, he would say publicly two years later, was "a blank check signed by the Congress in an atmosphere of urgency that seemed at the time to preclude debate.

"I myself, as chairman of the Foreign Relations Committee, served as floor manager of the Southeast Asia Resolution and did all I could to bring about its prompt and overwhelming adoption," he said. "I did so because I was confident that President Johnson would use our endorsement with wisdom and restraint. I was also influenced by partisanship: an election campaign was in progress and I had no wish to make any difficulties for the President in his race against a Republican candidate whose election I thought would be a disaster for the country."

Later, when he examined the available information, he would conclude that the announced second attack of the torpedo boats on the American vessels was, at the least, shrouded in doubt. He was left with an extremely uneasy feeling that it had been deliberately staged or set up by the Americans to gain public support for military action. After all, he had not sat in on the Bay of Pigs deliberations for nothing.[3]

Two years after the incident, Assistant Secretary of State William P. Bundy told the Foreign Relations Committee that he had prepared several contingent drafts of the Resolution some time before the Tonkin incidents. This led some Senators to wonder if the Administration had not merely been waiting for a chance to push through such a resolution at a time when Congress would not ask too many questions.

In November 1964, President Johnson won by an unprecedented margin over Senator Barry Goldwater, who many people feared was too warlike. Johnson, on the other hand, campaigned as a man who would take no rash actions. He said he did not intend to lead the United States into a wider war in Vietnam. "There are those" he proclaimed, "that say I ought to go north and drop bombs, to try to wipe out the supply lines, and they think that would escalate the war. But we don't want to get involved in a nation with seven hundred million people [China] and get tied down in a land war in Asia." [4]

While the American people were deciding the future of Lyndon Johnson (and thus their own), there were startling developments in the East. Nikita Khrushchev, who had dominated Russia for a decade, was suddenly toppled from power by other leaders of the Communist party. Why is not quite certain. Some have written that the reason was domestic, primarily the failure of his agricultural programs. Others feel it was his erratic foreign policy, one that proclaimed a belief in peaceful coexistence yet paradoxically climaxed with a nuclear confrontation. Whatever the reasons, Khrushchev's dismissal, although abrupt and announced in harshly critical terms, was far different than such a dismissal would have been in the Stalin years. As far as was known in the West, he was permitted to live with some comfort and dignity and was occasionally seen in public. This has been taken as another sign of the gradual liberalization of Soviet life. But this liberalization is uncertain and sporadic, as demonstrated by the continued repression, and sometimes imprisonment, of dissenters, particularly writers.

Khrushchev was succeeded jointly by two men: Leonid Brezhnev as head of the Communist party, and Alexei Kosygin as Premier. The Kremlin no doubt wanted two colorless bureaucrats after the earthy, unpredictable Khrushchev and hoped that with two-man rule neither could gain too much power.

Despite President Johnson's intentions, the war in South Vietnam was going badly and the situation steadily worsened. By early 1965 the Pentagon was convinced that if the United States did not intervene with substantial ground troops, the Viet Cong would conquer most of South Vietnam and topple the Saigon regime which had been weakened by coup after coup. So, on February 7, following a Viet Cong attack on American installations at Pleiku, Johnson ordered a step the Pentagon had long advocated: the bombing of North Vietnam. He also ordered step-by-step increases in the number of American troops in Vietnam—which by 1968 would reach over a half million. These forces were backed up by additional tens of thousands in nearby Thailand, from which air raids were launched against the enemy in both North and South Vietnam, and by a vast naval armada operating off the Vietnamese coast. As one high official put it: "It was almost imperceptible, the way we got in. There was no one move that you could call decisive, or irreversible, not even many actions that you could argue against in isolation. Yet when you put it all together, there we were in a war on the Asian mainland, with nobody really putting up much of a squawk while we were doing it." [5]

But there were squawks, particularly in the academic and intellectual communities. Years of unease over American policy were beginning to break out as open dissent, dissent that became so widespread as to convince Johnson in early 1968 that he should not stand for re-election. And in the early years, while dissent over Vietnam was beginning to grow, Johnson made another foreign policy move that also subjected him to severe criticism: the intervention in the Dominican Republic.

On April 24, 1965 a revolution erupted in that country. Its purpose was to restore to power the democratically elected Juan Bosch, who had been overthrown by a right-wing military junta. Just as the revolution was gaining momentum, Johnson decided the United States had to intervene. At first, on April 28, he announced that marines—an unwelcome symbol to Latin Americans who remembered marine landings in several countries early in the century—had landed to protect the lives of Americans in Santo Domingo. There was, to be sure, chaos in the city but critics of the Administration have argued that there was no great danger to Americans.

Then, on May 2, Johnson declared on television that American intervention was necessary because "a band of Communist conspirators" was taking control of what had begun as a "popular democratic revolution." He said that now 14,000 American troops had landed (the total was to reach 20,000) to "prevent another Communist state in this hemisphere." Yet even while American troops were taking the side of the military junta against the revolutionaries, President Johnson said in the same speech: "The form and nature of the free Dominican government, I assure you, is solely a matter for the Dominican Republic. . . . And neither we nor any other nation in the hemisphere can or should take it upon itself ever to interfere with the affairs of your country or any other country."

Again, American foreign policy had foundered on that basic question of whether or not the establishment of a Communist government was sufficient cause for American intervention in the domestic affairs of another nation. No matter what the answer, there seemed to be—even according to American statements—only a few Communists involved in the revolution.

The American action did succeed in establishing order in the Dominican Republic, although it is still too early to know what the long-term effects will be. But the short-term effects were clear: the United States was condemned and criticized the world over, and the intervention served to increase the anti-Administration protests within the United States.

The rest of Johnson's term was dominated by Vietnam and the opposition to the war there. During the first year or two in office, Johnson had pushed through Congress an extraordinary amount of liberal legislation, legislation that had eluded Kennedy. It seemed then that Johnson was on his way to making an imposing, perhaps even historic record, but gradually he became preoccupied with the war. He turned away from domestic matters at a time when the relations between whites and blacks were worsening, when the problems of the cities were multiplying, and the term "generation gap" was used so often it became a cliché. His mind and energy were devoted to the war, along with tens of billions of dollars that otherwise could have been directed toward domestic programs.

Over the Christmas holidays in 1965 Johnson conducted what was termed a "peace offensive." He halted the bombing of North Vietnam for thirty-seven days—critics had long said that if he stopped the bombing, there could be peace talks—and sent high-ranking emissaries all over the world. But he still refused to deal with the Viet Cong, the main adversary of

the Saigon regime and Washington, so the pause ended without result and the war grew more intense. And so it went all
through 1966, with occasional flurries of hope that soon
vanished. The number of American troops grew, American
casualties increased, and peace seemed as elusive as ever.

Johnson sincerely wanted peace and presumably so did
the Viet Cong and North Vietnam, but neither side was able
to accept the conditions of the other. By January 1, 1967
American troops had reached a strength of 380,000. American commanders continued to say that the tide of battle had
turned in favor of the United States, but still the war went
on, with the Viet Cong suffering terrible losses. Eventually
these losses—and the increased American commitment—
caused Ho Chi Minh to send North Vietnamese troops into
the war. At first there had been few if any regular North
Vietnamese troops in the South. But American escalation—
each new step was supposed to tilt the balance permanently
in favor of the United States—was somehow matched by the
enemy, who fought without air support, without transport,
hitting hard, then melting away into the hills or jungles.

In February 1967 attention was diverted from Vietnam
briefly by a whole series of disclosures that the CIA had
penetrated a number of American domestic organizations:
the National Students Association and more than thirty
groups in the fields of labor, journalism, education, law, and
religion. Some defended this as necessary to defend America
against Communism; others have argued that it was repre-
hensible that groups purporting to be independent were
actually influenced or directed by the undercover arm of the
government, an agency that by law was supposed to operate
only overseas. The former said it was one of the unfortunate

facts of life in the Cold War; the latter asserted that it was a demonstration of how the Cold War had undermined American institutions.

The widespread furor caused by the CIA revelations was another sign of the constantly growing dissent against the Vietnam War. Part of the dissent was based on the belief that the United States was wrong to intervene in a civil war on the side of a repressive, unrepresentative oligarchy, part on the belief that the war was costing too high a price in money that could be used for programs desperately needed at home, too high a cost in domestic turmoil, and, of course, too high a price in American lives.

At the beginning of 1967 the American deaths in Vietnam since January 1, 1961 totaled 6664, whereas by November 11, 1967, less than eleven months later, the figure had more than doubled, to 14,621 dead with another 91,971 wounded.[6] And the number of deaths was to double yet again in 1968, so that by the end of President Johnson's Administration the deaths had climbed to over 30,000, approaching the death toll in the Korean War, 33,629.

However, despite the spreading dissent, the Johnson Administration continued to argue that it was North Vietnam that was prolonging the war by its refusal to stop its "aggression" in the South. North Vietnam rejected this argument and continued to assert that there could be peace talks if the United States unconditionally halted the bombing of North Vietnam.

One of those occasional flurries of hope came in late June of 1967 when Johnson met for two days with Russian Premier Kosygin, who had come to New York to attend the special session of the UN General Assembly called after the 6-day

Arab-Israeli war. Kosygin would not go to Washington to visit Johnson and Johnson would not go to New York to visit Kosygin, so they finally settled on the little town of Glassboro, New Jersey, about halfway between. The meeting was reportedly cordial but there was no progress on Vietnam.

On September 12 Defense Secretary Robert McNamara announced that the United States would build a "thin" anti-missile network able to defend against any intercontinental ballistic missile force the People's Republic of China might be able to develop in the next ten years. (China had successfully tested her first hydrogen bomb in June.) McNamara stressed that the United States did not want to intensify the arms race with Russia but was building the "limited" anti-ballistic missile (ABM) system because "there is evidence that the Chinese are devoting substantial resources to the development of both nuclear warheads and missile delivery systems . . . one can conceive of conditions under which China might miscalculate."

This seemed to agree with the thinking of Secretary of State Dean Rusk, who asserted in a press conference on October 12 that the United States had to keep its commitments in Vietnam and Southeast Asia and that failure to do so would "subject this country to mortal danger." He then drew an ominous picture of the next decade as one in which a billion Chinese armed with nuclear weapons would threaten all of Asia and imperil the security of the United States.

Critics of the Administration dismissed the contentions of both Secretaries, arguing that the establishment of a "thin" ABM system would lead its supporters to insist that a "thick" shield was essential for national security. This in turn, the critics said, would cause the Russians to take similar action, raising the already enormous costs of the arms race to astronomical proportions. Unresolved through 1968, the issue was one of the major decisions left for the Nixon Administration.

As 1967 drew to a close with no end to the war in sight, there began to be reports that Senator Eugene McCarthy, a liberal Democrat from Minnesota, might enter primaries in 1968 to try to block the renomination of President Johnson. McCarthy, who had become a leading critic of the Vietnam War, said in Boston on November 11 that party leaders who disagreed with the Johnson policy "have an obligation to speak out and party unity is not a sufficient excuse for their silence."

Another leading critic, Senator Robert F. Kennedy, brother of the late President, said a few days later that if McCarthy were to enter the primaries, "it would be a healthy influence on the Democratic party." But he continued to assert that he would not challenge the President, although many critics of the war had been urging him to do so.

Despite the growing dissent, however, political experts were almost unanimous in their belief that although Johnson might be defeated in the Presidential election, he could not be deprived of his party's nomination. An incumbent President, they said, was simply too powerful to be unseated within his party.

During these weeks of ferment the Administration tried to counter the belief that there was no end of the war in sight. On November 19 General William Westmoreland, the American commander in Vietnam, said: "We are winning a war of attrition," and he predicted that within two years or less we would be able to "phase down the level of our military effort." Yet despite the heavy losses the Viet Cong and the North Vietnamese had suffered, there was widespread skepticism that the United States was winning the war, for American spokesmen had been making similar statements for years, statements that were often followed by requests for more troops to meet urgent needs.

General Westmoreland was summoned back to Washington during the year-end holiday season and made a number of public appearances, including some on nationwide radio and television, in which he repeated his optimistic statements. Then, on January 30, 1968, the Viet Cong and the North Vietnamese struck all over South Vietnam in their now-famous Tet offensive. On the first day of what was supposed to be a lunar New Year truce, the enemy hit thirty provincial capitals, occupied most of Hué, the ancient capital, and for days held parts of Saigon, including, for a few hours, buildings of the U.S. Embassy. On February 2 Johnson called the offensive "a complete failure" both militarily and psychologically. Doubtless the enemy did not accomplish all it intended, but the scope and strength of the Tet offensive did have a profound effect on the American public, shaking even further its confidence in the Administration's Vietnam policy.

Also in January there began a chain of events that within months would demonstrate in startling fashion that all was not well within the Communist world either. On January 25, 1968 after a bitter intra-party struggle, the longtime Stalinist leader of the Czech Communist party, Antonin Novotny, was ousted in favor of the more liberal Alexander Dubček. Dubček soon launched a program of liberalization in Czech life, a program that was enthusiastically welcomed by his countrymen. Nonetheless, Czechoslovakia remained firmly within the Communist camp and despite increasing protests by the Kremlin about the pace of liberalization, Dubček and his colleagues insisted that they were loyal Communists and would remain so.

Americans gave passing glances to the developing situation in Czechoslovakia, but they were preoccupied with the extraordinary political developments at home. Eugene McCarthy did announce that he would challenge the President in a number of Democratic primaries, an almost incredible decision. The first primary was in New Hampshire, and during the wintry days of January and February McCarthy crisscrossed the state supported by swelling ranks of young people, mainly from colleges, who went from door to door politely pleading the antiwar cause. The experts said McCarthy didn't have a chance and the newspapers were filled with stories of how disastrously his campaign was being run.

Also during January the Administration received another severe blow. On January 23 an American intelligence ship, the *Pueblo,* was captured by four North Korean patrol boats. North Korea claimed the *Pueblo* was within the 12-mile territorial limit, while the United States insisted it was in international waters outside the limit. Whichever, North Korea took the ship into harbor and held the crew (originally eighty-three but one was killed in the seizure) for almost a year until January 1969. Then, in an unprecedented diplomatic maneuver, the United States obtained the release of the men—but not the ship—by handing over to North Korea a written admission that the *Pueblo* was within North Korean waters. Before handing over the admission, though, the United States proclaimed that the allegations were not true, that it was admitting guilt only to free the crew.

At the time of the seizure it seemed as if a major international crisis were developing. On January 24 Dean Rusk said it was "in a category of actions to be construed as an act of war." And the next day Johnson ordered to duty nearly 15,000 Navy and Air Force reservists, and in a show of strength shifted a task force including the nuclear-powered aircraft carrier *Enterprise* to waters off the North Korean coast.

However, despite widespread demands that the United States "do something about the *Pueblo*," there was little Johnson could do. American military strength was already severely extended in Vietnam and even if it had not been, any strong American response would have involved considerable military and political risk. In addition, the Administration was at the time already under severe criticism at home and abroad for a foreign policy that was termed too adventurous. It believed, correctly, that sooner or later the men would be released, that the capture was simply one of those unfortunate incidents of the Cold War.

The significance of the *Pueblo* incident, dramatic as it was, was little compared to the impact of the New Hampshire primary. Eugene McCarthy did not win. He received 42 per cent of the vote compared to 48 per cent for Johnson, who, although not on the ballot, had been supported by an organized, well-financed write-in campaign. Nonetheless, almost everyone interpreted the result as an enormous psychological victory for McCarthy and the antiwar forces, and it began to appear that McCarthy might well defeat Johnson in some of the later primaries. Four days later, on March 16, Senator Robert Kennedy declared that he, too, was a candidate, reversing a stand he had taken on many occasions.

But the biggest surprise of all came on the night of March 31 when in the last sentence of a televised speech on Vietnam Johnson said, "I shall not seek, and I will not accept the nomination of my party for another term as your President." No doubt Johnson was greatly influenced by the results of the New Hampshire primary and the certainty that further primary struggles involving him against both Senators Mc-Carthy and Kennedy would seriously, perhaps fatally, weaken the Democratic party for the fall election. Further, Johnson was deeply convinced that his Vietnam policy was right and he felt that by removing himself from the political arena, no one, in Vietnam or at home, could think he had political motivations in any moves he made. For in that same speech he announced that the United States would stop the bombing of most of North Vietnam (although in fact increasing it in the remaining areas) and asked the enemy to respond in some way that could bring peace talks nearer.

North Vietnam quickly replied and on April 3 offered to meet with the United States to discuss the unconditional end to the bombing of all North Vietnam, still its condition for full-fledged peace talks. For weeks the two sides bickered over a site for the talks but finally agreed on Paris, and the talks began on May 13. However, Hanoi continued to insist on a complete bombing halt and the inclusion of the Na-tional Liberation Front (Viet Cong) as full participants in any subsequent talks. The deadlock lasted for months, until just days before the Presidential election of November 5, when Johnson announced a complete halt in the bombing, an announcement that must surely have helped Vice President Humphrey, Richard Nixon's opponent.

Vietnam and the election campaign were inextricably intertwined. Richard Nixon easily won the Republican nomination over his chief competition, Governor Nelson Rockefeller of New York, but it was a far different story in the Democratic party. Although Vice President Hubert Humphrey announced his candidacy soon after President Johnson withdrew, the announcement came too late for him to enter any of the state primaries. Thus, Senators McCarthy and Kennedy, both antiwar candidates, competed against one another.

Kennedy, because of the luster of the family name and the powerful political organization that remained from his brother's days—plus, of course, his own personal popularity —was the favorite. He won handily in Indiana, then lost to McCarthy in Oregon. The issue seemed to swing on the most populous state, California. Both Kennedy and McCarthy were popular there, with Kennedy a distinct favorite. He did win narrowly, 46 per cent to 42, but savored his victory only for minutes. Shortly after midnight on June 5, he was fatally wounded by an assassin, less than five years after his brother was murdered in Dallas and only two months after Martin Luther King was shot in Memphis. Again the course of American history was changed by an assassin's bullet, for the chances were good that Kennedy would have won the Democratic nomination and gone on to defeat Nixon in the November election.

But that is only speculation. Another Kennedy was dead, only McCarthy was left to carry on the antiwar fight, and he was completely unacceptable to many regular party leaders; whereas Kennedy, despite challenging Johnson, had close political ties with many of those same leaders. Thus, it was no surprise when Vice President Humphrey won the nomination on August 27. What was surprising was the turmoil that attended the convention. Chicago police clashed violently with antiwar demonstrators, turning the streets and parks into battlegrounds and creating a spectacle of violence that shocked the American public. Although Mayor Richard J. Daley defended the police action as necessary to preserve law and order, an impartial study group drew up a report harshly critical of police behavior.

Even while the Democrats were choosing their candidate, extraordinary events were taking place in Eastern Europe. For months the Kremlin had been attacking publicly the new Czech government, terming its liberalization program as counterrevolutionary and making the absurd accusation that the West was somehow responsible. Even as this condemnation grew, observers in the West almost unanimously believed that Russia would not resort to military intervention. They all agreed that the days of Hungary were forever gone. They were terribly wrong.

On August 20, 200,000 Russian troops, augmented by token forces of other members of the Soviet-controlled Warsaw Pact, marched without warning into Czechoslovakia. The Czechs, perhaps remembering the brutal days of Hungary, did not offer armed resistance but instead undertook a passive resistance that the Russians did not quite know how to cope with. By the end of a week the troops occupying the country were increased to 650,000. And, as in Hungary, the Russians seized the leaders of the government, Party First Secretary Dubček and three other liberal Communists.

For a while the world feared they would meet the same deadly fate as Imre Nagy, but the Russians seemed no longer prepared to go that far. Czechoslovakia's President, the war hero Ludvik Svoboda, flew to Moscow and convinced the

Russians to free Dubček, insisting that no settlement was possible unless Dubček and the others were free to participate in the discussions. Whatever the reasons—perhaps the Kremlin was influenced by the outcry the world over, including condemnation by the leaders of many Communist parties in the West—the Russians gave in. Dubček and the others were free again but there was little they could achieve in the talks; under the shadow of Russian tanks, they had to agree to end much of the liberalization program and fire many liberal officials.

Svoboda, Dubček, and the others returned to Prague, but it was a different Czechoslovakia than the one they had left the week before. Now the men who had led the liberalization had to undo their own works or be replaced by pro-Soviet Czechs who would have no interest in salvaging whatever they could. Subsequent months were painful. Passive resistance continued as liberal Czech officials were forced to crack down on their own people, who in turn began to criticize the very leaders who had been heroes a few short months before.

A tragic symbol of Czechoslovakia's dilemma was the death of Jan Palach, a young Czech who in January 1969 set himself ablaze in protest. Taking his life in the very same way the Buddhists in Vietnam had protested the repressive Saigon government, he became a martyr and thousands of people streamed by his coffin to demonstrate their solidarity against the Russian-imposed repression.

Perhaps one day the world will know why the Russians marched into Czechoslovakia. Were they afraid that the liberalization in Czechoslovakia was a step toward the disintegration of the Russian Empire in Eastern Europe? Did they believe that developments in Czechoslovakia would make them more vulnerable to some possible attack from West Germany? Did they fear that liberalization would spread to their own people and mean that the Kremlin would be faced with a choice between major concessions, concessions that might cause the situation to get out of hand, or harsh repression?

No matter what the reason, the invasion was a monumental blunder. Instead of strengthening their position in Eastern Europe, the Russians weakened it, for Czechoslovakia was no longer a willing ally but a resentful occupied country. They made enemies out of friends, for as Dubček said, tears streaming down his cheek as he learned of the Russian invasion, "I have devoted my entire life to cooperation with the Soviet Union, and they have done this to me. It is my personal tragedy." [7]

The intervention demonstrated to the world that often-expressed Russian words about self-determination were the worst kind of hypocrisy, that they believed in only one definition of Communism, Moscow's. It also represented a major setback in the Russian campaign to appear as a peace-loving nation, a campaign that had prospered because of the widespread criticism of America's intervention in the Dominican Republic and, especially, Vietnam.

And perhaps it meant one more thing: that the momentum toward liberalization in Eastern Europe is really irresistible, that it can be halted (and then just temporarily) only by the kind of brutal and complete repression used in Hungary—and that even mighty Russia hesitates to go that far now.

The Russian invasion of Czechoslovakia, which ten years before would have had a profound effect on the American electorate, was taken pretty much in stride during the 1968 campaign. Perhaps after Korea and Hungary and Suez and the Congo and Cuba and the Dominican Republic and Vietnam, Americans could no longer be shocked. The big question of the campaign was whether the majority Democratic party could hold together in the face of the widespread dissatisfaction with the Vietnam War, particularly after the tumultuous and divisive convention in Chicago. Nixon was a heavy favorite, not so much for himself but because few thought that Vice President Humphrey, who had long supported the Vietnam War, could successfully carry such a political burden.

At first it seemed there would be no contest because of the great defection of Democratic supporters of McCarthy and Kennedy, and because many labor union members in the North were expected to vote for the third-party candidate, George Wallace, a Southern segregationist. But Humphrey waged a vigorous campaign, many antiwar Democrats came back to the party, however reluctantly, and Wallace seemed to hurt Nixon more, carrying five Southern states that would otherwise have gone to the Republican. The race was so close that it was not until the morning following election day that Nixon's narrow victory became certain. But he had won only 43.4 per cent of the popular vote, just a fraction of a percentage point more than Humphrey, while Wallace received 13.5 per cent. The Democrats continued to dominate the Senate and the House of Representatives.

Thus, when President Nixon took office on January 20, 1969, he did so with the narrowest mandate in more than half a century. This at a time when the nation faced a whole range of agonizing problems. Not only did Nixon have to seek solutions to such monumental domestic difficulties as the relations between blacks and whites and the often-related financial and social problems of the big cities (not a major one of which, incidentally, was carried by Nixon), but there were a host of foreign problems as well.

Foremost was the war in Vietnam which continued to defy easy solution. Then Nixon was faced with decisions affecting American relations with Russia and China; he had to decide whether or not to go ahead with the "thin" anti-ballistic missile system. And there were other decisions affecting NATO, the Middle East, Cuba and all of Latin America, and, basic to all these, the philosophy that underlay American foreign policy.

Would Nixon, who made his reputation as a tough anti-Communist, follow the same tough anti-Communist line that had been followed by Truman, Eisenhower, Kennedy, and Johnson, or would he decide that the time had come to adopt a more flexible stance, to seek a fundamental accommodation with the Russians and perhaps even the Chinese? Would he continue to act according to the long-term American belief that American security was significantly affected by events anywhere in the world, or would he decide that the United States would be better served if it let developing countries seek their own political and economic solutions, even left-wing or Communist, without attempting to enforce American influence by overt or covert means?

Would he continue to believe, as do many Americans, that the United States has a mission to lead the world, that it was, in effect, the world's policeman? Or would he decide that America could best influence the world by demonstrating that it could solve its own immense domestic problems, that its political and economic systems could successfully cope with the stresses and strains of the modern world?

These are not easy decisions, for it is difficult for any President to change a foreign policy that has behind it the momentum of a quarter-century. The military-industrial complex has grown stronger, not less so, since President Eisenhower gave his historic warning in 1961, and this powerful complex is convinced that the expenditure of enormous sums of money, constantly growing sums, is necessary to ensure the nation's security. The nation itself has been conditioned to believe in the necessity, even the moral obligation of a hard anti-Communist policy, but there are increasing numbers who have been convinced by the Vietnam War that rigid, inflexible adherence to such a policy does more harm than good. For it is hard to see how American intervention in Vietnam has in any way weakened the Russian or Chinese Communists, and there is ample evidence that the intervention has had profoundly deleterious effects on the United States itself.

This then is the context in which Richard Milhous Nixon assumed the terrible burdens of the Presidency. Not until 1973 at the earliest will we be able to judge how well he has done.

Epilogue

AT THIS writing the Cold War is not yet over, nor is it possible to predict when it will end. But the possibilities for an early end are better than ever, even if only because both sides—or perhaps there are now three sides—are tired of it. Although President Nixon can do much to end it, he cannot end it alone. For that, Russia and China must cooperate.

Since the Cold War is not over, any judgments may be premature. But perhaps a few observations can be ventured. Although there are writers who like to blame one side or the other for starting the Cold War, it may be nearer the truth to suggest that it was predictable given the circumstances and the participants.

At the end of the Second World War Russia was terribly weak, had suffered terrible losses. Most Americans forget that the Soviet Union lost some 25,000,000 people in the war compared to just over 400,000 for the United States. Russia, terrified not only by the recent horror but by its own ideolog-

175

ical conviction that capitalism must of necessity oppose it, felt desperately vulnerable and concluded that safety lay only in the establishment of a barrier of buffer states between it and the West, particularly Germany. And with its victorious armies standing unchallenged in the prostrate nations of Eastern Europe, the opportunity was there to create such a barrier, and the opportunity also to bring the "blessings" of Communism to the peoples of these ravaged nations.

Perhaps Stalin's Russia could have acted in no other way. But just as natural was the West's response to the clamping down of the Iron Curtain. Albeit genuinely distressed by the loss of freedom of these nations, the West, no less than the Russians, was also victimized by its own ideology. It saw Communism as a mortal enemy. It remembered the terrible Stalinist purges of the 30's; it saw the repressive society of the Soviet Union; it saw the imposition of Russian rule over all of Eastern Europe; and so it was easy for the West to see as aggressive, expansionist, what the Russians saw as defensive. Thus, the action of one led to the reaction of the other, which led to the further reaction of the first, and so on and so on in a tragic spiral.

Added to the perfectly legitimate skepticism with which the United States regarded Soviet Russia, and compounding the misunderstanding that followed, was a moralistic tendency inherited from the Puritans who both founded this country and established its ethic. Americans have always tended to see conflicts in terms of good and evil. They did in the First World War under Wilson; they did in the Second under Roosevelt; and when the Russians ceased to be allies and became enemies instead, they became identified with evil. They were no longer Russians, a people, but Communists, evildoers.

As the competition between the United States and Russia intensified, it was not seen as the perfectly normal competition between two great powers but as an ethical struggle between Democracy and Communism. Thus, any accommodation with Russia—no matter whether in the mutual interest of both countries or not—was seen as a compromise with evil, a conviction that was intensified under the profoundly moralistic John Foster Dulles and his brother, Allen, head of the CIA.

But crusades are seldom conducted on entirely rational terms (all this applies to the Russians as well, although they often seem more successful at putting national considerations before ideological), and frequently it seemed that the United States chose a course of action based more on how anti-Communist it was rather than how it served the real interests of the country. It is difficult to understand, for instance, how American interventions in Cuba, the Dominican Republic, and Vietnam have helped the United States. Indeed, just the contrary seems to be true.

However, there are many who would profoundly disagree with this analysis and who would argue that America's safety was dependent on opposing Communism whenever and wherever it appeared. Perhaps they are right. Only time will tell.

Notes

CHAPTER 1   THE BEGINNING

1. Walter LaFeber, *America, Russia, and the Cold War, 1945–1966*, p. 7. I have relied heavily on LaFeber in the early part of this book. (For complete information on all books referred to in these notes, see the Bibliography.)
2. John Spanier, *American Foreign Policy Since World War II*, p. 1.
3. LaFeber, p. 6.

CHAPTER 2   GROWING TENSIONS

1. Richard J. Barnet, *Intervention and Revolution*, p. 65.
2. LaFeber, p. 19.
3. LaFeber, p. 21.
4. John Lukacs, *A New History of the Cold War*, pp. 63, 65.
5. Adam B. Ulam, *Expansion and Coexistence*, p. 475.
6. *New York Times*, March 6, 1946. Text on p. 4.
7. LaFeber, p. 38.

CHAPTER 3   THE POINT OF NO RETURN

1. Lukacs, p. 82.
2. Spanier, p. 34.
3. Harry S. Truman, *Memoirs: Years of Trial and Hope*, Vol. II, p. 128.
4. Truman, p. 130.
5. Barnet, p. 121. In his book Barnet gives a superb critical account of the decision to establish the Truman Doctrine.

6. Joseph M. Jones, *The Fifteen Weeks,* 1964.

7. Barnet, p. 116.

8. Quotations from S. G. Xydis, *Greece and the Great Powers,* Thessaloniki, 1963, cited by Barnet, p. 117.

9. Barnet, p. 125.

10. Major Edgar O'Ballance, *The Greek Civil War, 1944–1949,* New York, Praeger, 1966.

11. LaFeber, p. 46; Barnet, p. 120.

CHAPTER 4   THE MARSHALL PLAN AND CONTAINMENT

1. Spanier, LaFeber, and Carleton all discuss this question, and Carleton especially gives a good concise account of the Marshall Plan. William G. Carleton, *The Revolution in American Foreign Policy.*

2. *New York Times,* July 3, 1947. Text on p. 3.

3. Spanier, p. 46.

4. Carleton, p. 169.

5. George F. Kennan, *Memoirs 1925–1950,* p. 319.

6. Kennan, p. 320.

7. Kennan, p. 321.

8. Kennan, p. 322.

9. LaFeber, p. 62.

CHAPTER 5   CONFRONTATION

1. W. Phillips Davidson, *The Berlin Blockade.* A useful, greatly detailed account of the blockade written from a pro-American point of view.

2. Davidson, p. 124.

CHAPTER 6   THE CLOSING OF THE RING

1. LaFeber, p. 77.

2. Spanier, p. 85.

CHAPTER 7   FROM CONFRONTATION TO WAR

1. In the following pages I have relied heavily on the admirably detailed *Korea: The Limited War* by David Rees.

2. Rees, p. 25.

3. Rees, p. 99.

4. State Department Bulletin, December 18, 1950.

5. Ulam, p. 504.

6. A good discussion of this question is given in Carleton, p. 232 and following.

7. Carleton, p. 232.

8. For an account of Stevenson's years (1961–65) as Ambassador to the United Nations, see my *The Remnants of Power: The Tragic Last Years of Adlai Stevenson.*

CHAPTER 8 THE DULLES CRUSADE

1. LaFeber, p. 144.

2. A concise but detailed account of this coup is given in Barnet, pp. 225–229.

3. Barnet, p. 225.

4. Although there have been many first-rate accounts of the American intervention in Vietnam, perhaps the most superbly documented is *The United States in Vietnam* by George McTurnan Kahin and John W. Lewis.

5. Kahin and Lewis, p. 50.

6. Kahin and Lewis, p. 61.

7. Barnet, p. 232.

8. Spanier, p. 136.

9. Carleton, p. 225.

10. Ulam, p. 561.

CHAPTER 9 THAT INCREDIBLE YEAR

1. Ulam, p. 581.

2. LaFeber, p. 188.

3. Lukacs, p. 140. Lukacs' account of the Hungarian revolution is both detailed and moving.

4. Lukacs, p. 143.

CHAPTER 10 EISENHOWER'S FINAL TERM

1. LaFeber, p. 200.

2. LaFeber, p. 200.

3. A brief but detailed account of the Lebanese intervention is given in Barnet, pp. 132–152.

4. Carleton, p. 333.

5. Spanier, p. 16.

6. LaFeber, p. 203.

7. Carleton, p. 278.

CHAPTER 11   THE KENNEDY YEARS

1. Text in the *New York Times*, January 18, 1961.
2. The Bay of Pigs and the subsequent Cuban missile crisis have been discussed in great detail by two top Kennedy aides: Arthur M. Schlesinger, Jr. in *A Thousand Days*; and Theodore C. Sorenson in *Kennedy*. The two Cuban crises are examined from a different point of view in my *The Remnants of Power*. Both the Schlesinger and Sorenson books are essential to a knowledge of the Kennedy Administration.
3. Philip Geyelin, *Lyndon B. Johnson and the World*, pp. 35–40.
4. Barnet, p. 212.
5. A good, concise discussion of the Laos crisis is in Carleton, pp. 316–320.
6. Walton, p. 38.
7. First-hand reports of these meetings have been made by Sorenson, and by Robert F. Kennedy in *Thirteen Days*.
8. Walton, p. 56.
9. Schlesinger, p. 909.

CHAPTER 12   THE JOHNSON YEARS

1. It may well be that, if he had lived, Kennedy would have reversed his policy in Vietnam. Schlesinger (p. 927) has written that the young President was planning to accept Rusk's resignation after the 1964 election and seek a new Secretary; such an act—since Rusk was identified with the Kennedy Vietnam policy—would have indicated at least some degree of change. Walt Rostow, however, has disputed this, saying that Kennedy would have been as tough or tougher.
2. *New York Times*, January 1 and 2, 1964.
3. Haynes Johnson and Bernard M. Gwertzman, *Fulbright: The Dissenter*, p. 199.
4. Geyelin, p. 195.
5. Geyelin, p. 213.
6. Department of Defense figures.
7. *New York Times*, September 2, 1968, p. 1.

Important Dates
in the Cold War

1945

FEB. 3–11	Yalta Conference
APRIL 12	President Roosevelt dies
APRIL 25	American and Russian armies meet along the Elbe River
JULY 16	First A-Bomb exploded at Alamogordo, N.M.
JULY 17	Potsdam Conference
AUG. 6	U.S. drops A-Bomb on Hiroshima, three days later on Nagasaki
AUG. 8	Russia joins war against Japan
DEC. 5	General Marshall's mission to China

1946

FEB. 6	Stalin's tough Cold War speech
FEBRUARY	Marshall gets agreement between Nationalists and Communists in China but it collapses by mid-April
MARCH 5	Churchill's Iron Curtain speech
NOVEMBER	Ho Chi Minh begins rebellion in Vietnam

1947

MARCH 12   Truman proposes what comes to be known as the
             Truman Doctrine
JUNE 5   Marshall proposes plan to rebuild Europe

1948

FEB. 25   Czechoslovakia falls into Russian bloc
MARCH 17   Britain, France, and the Benelux nations sign
             Brussels Pact that is forerunner of NATO
JUNE 24   Russians begin Berlin blockade
JUNE 26   Truman orders Berlin airlift
JUNE 28   Break between Stalin and Tito made public

1949

APRIL 4   NATO Pact signed
SEPT. 23   Truman announces that Russia has A-Bomb
OCT. 1   Communists proclaim People's Republic of
             China

1950

JAN. 12   Acheson says Korea outside U.S. defense perim-
             eter
JUNE 25   North Korea invades South Korea
JUNE 30   U.S. ground forces join conflict
SEPTEMBER   Acheson startles Allies by saying West Germany
             must be rearmed
SEPT. 15   Amphibious landings at Inchon begin to turn
             tide in Korea
SEPT. 30   U.S. troops regain 38th parallel
OCT. 7   UN sanctions military unification of Korea
NOV. 20   U.S. forces reach Chinese border despite Chinese
             warnings that MacArthur dismisses as bluff
NOV. 26   Chinese "volunteers" hit Americans, force retreat

1951

FEB. 1	UN names China aggressor
MARCH	U.S. recovers from Chinese onslaught, again regains 38th parallel
APRIL 11	Truman fires MacArthur

1952

MARCH	Russia proposes negotiations about Germany but U.S. declines
MAY	U.S. and Britain pledge to keep troops in Europe indefinitely to lessen fears of German participation in Western alliance
AUTUMN	Republicans in Presidential campaign promise to "roll back" the Iron Curtain
NOV. 1	U.S. explodes first hydrogen device at Eniwetok Atoll in Pacific Ocean

1953

MARCH 5	Stalin dies
MARCH	Churchill sees chance for post-Stalin thaw; Dulles not interested
JUNE 17	Riots against regime in East Germany. Soviet troops put them down
JULY 27	Korean Armistice signed

1954

APRIL–JULY	Geneva Conference on Indochina
MAY	Dienbienphu falls; U.S. refuses to send military help
JUNE	CIA coup overthrows Guatemalan government
AUG. 12	Russia explodes first hydrogen device
SEPT. 8	SEATO Pact
OCT. 23	Germany enters Western Alliance

DEC. 2   U.S. and Nationalist China (Formosa) sign Mutual Defense Treaty

1955

FEB. 24   Baghdad Pact (later CENTO) completes ring around Sino-Soviet periphery

MAY 5   West Germany becomes sovereign; with Italy formally joins NATO

MAY 14   Warsaw Pact. Communist response to NATO

MAY 15   Austrian State Treaty

JULY 18–23   Summit conference in Geneva

1956

FEB. 24   Khrushchev startles Communist world by denouncing Stalin

JUNE 28   Uprising in Poznan, Poland. Gomulka released

JULY 19   Dulles announces U.S. will not finance Aswan Dam in Egypt

JULY 26   Nasser seizes Suez Canal

OCT. 19–21   Polish Communists defy Russia, elect Gomulka

OCT. 23   Hungarian revolt; Russian Empire seems to be collapsing but then Khrushchev takes brutal measures to end revolt

OCT. 29   Israel invades Egypt; Britain and France join the next day

NOV. 7   Middle East fighting stops after both U.S. and Soviet Union condemn it

1957

OCT. 4   Sputnik

1958

MARCH 31   Khrushchev announces unilateral moratorium on nuclear testing

JULY 15   Eisenhower sends troops to Lebanon

AUGUST   Eisenhower announces U.S. moratorium on testing; United Kingdom follows suit

NOVEMBER   Russian "ultimatum" on Berlin

1959

JAN. 1   Castro takes over in Cuba

APRIL   Dulles retires, dies a month later

SEPT. 15   Khrushchev visits U.S. for nearly two weeks

1960

MAY 1   U.S. U-2 shot down over Russia

MAY 16   Paris summit canceled

SEPTEMBER   Ho Chi Minh approves violent overthrow of South Vietnamese regime

DEC. 20   National Liberation Front established in South Vietnam

1961

JAN. 3   U.S. breaks relations with Cuba seventeen days before Kennedy takes office

APRIL 17   Bay of Pigs invasion

JUNE 3–4   Kennedy and Khrushchev meet in Vienna

JULY   Kennedy calls up reserves as Berlin tension grows

AUG. 13   Communists build Berlin Wall

SEPT. 1   Russia ends moratorium with massive nuclear tests. World protests

SEPT. 5   Kennedy announces U.S. to conduct underground tests

OCT. 30   Russia explodes 50-megaton bomb

1962

MARCH   Kennedy announces U.S. to resume atmospheric tests

OCT. 22   Kennedy shocks U.S. by announcing that Russian missile bases are being built in Cuba

OCT. 27–28   After days of agonizing tension, Khrushchev agrees to remove missile bases, Kennedy agrees not to invade Cuba

1963

JUNE 10   Kennedy's historic American University speech in which he says U.S. must re-examine its Cold War attitude

AUG. 5   Moscow Treaty to end nuclear testing except underground

NOV. 1   Diem regime overthrown in South Vietnam; Diem killed

NOV. 22   Kennedy assassinated

1964

JANUARY   Johnson decides to increase U.S. forces in Vietnam

AUG. 4   U.S. bomb North Vietnam after Tonkin Gulf incidents

AUG. 7   Congress passes Tonkin Resolution

OCT. 14   Khrushchev bloodlessly ousted; succeeded by Brezhnev and Kosygin

OCT. 16   China successfully tests first A-Bomb

1965

FEB. 7   U.S. bombs North Vietnam after Pleiku incident

MARCH 2   U.S. begins regular bombing of North Vietnam

APRIL 28   U.S. intervenes in the Dominican Republic

1966

JAN. 13   U.S. resumes bombing of North Vietnam after 37-day pause

JULY 1   France withdraws forces from integrated NATO command but stays in alliance

1967

JAN. 1   U.S. troops in Vietnam up to 380,000

JAN. 5   North Vietnam says talks possible if bombing stops

FEB. 13   CIA scandal; had penetrated U.S. domestic organizations

JUNE 17   China explodes first H-Bomb

JUNE 23–25   Johnson and Kosygin meet in Glassboro, N.J.

1968

JAN. 23   North Korea seizes the *Pueblo*

JAN. 25   Alexander Dubček assumes leadership of the Czech Communist party

JAN. 30   The Viet Cong launch the Tet offensive

MARCH 31   Johnson announces he will not seek re-election; orders partial bombing halt

MAY   U.S.-North Vietnam talks begin in Paris

AUG. 20   Russian troops occupy Czechoslovakia

NOV. 1   U.S. stops all bombing of North Vietnam

NOV. 5   Nixon defeats Humphrey

Bibliography

Barnet, Richard J., *Intervention and Revolution*. New York, New American Library, 1968.

Carleton, William G., *The Revolution in American Foreign Policy*. New York, Random House, 1967.

Davidson, W. Phillips, *The Berlin Blockade*. Princeton, N.J., Princeton University Press, 1958.

Evans, Rowland, and Novak, Robert, *Lyndon B. Johnson: The Exercise of Power*. New York, New American Library, 1966.

Fall, Bernard, *Anatomy of a Crisis: The Laotian Crisis of 1960–1961*. Garden City, N.Y., Doubleday, 1969.

Geyelin, Philip, *Lyndon B. Johnson and the World*. New York, Praeger, 1966.

Graebner, Norman A., *Cold War Diplomacy 1945–1960*. Princeton, N.J., Anvil, 1962.

Halle, Louis J., *The Cold War As History*. New York, Harper & Row, 1967.

Johnson, Haynes, and Gwertzman, Bernard M., *Fulbright: The Dissenter*. Garden City, N.Y., Doubleday, 1968.

Jones, Joseph M., *The Fifteen Weeks*. New York, Harcourt, Brace and World, 1964.

191

Kahin, George McTurnan, and Lewis, John W., *The United States in Vietnam*. New York, Delta, 1967.

Kennan, George F., *Memoirs 1925–1950*. Boston, Atlantic–Little, Brown, 1967.

Kennedy, Robert F., *Thirteen Days*. New York, Norton, 1968.

LaFeber, Walter, *America, Russia and the Cold War, 1945–1966*. New York, John Wiley & Sons, 1967.

Lukacs, John, *A New History of the Cold War*. Garden City, N.Y., Doubleday Anchor, 1966.

Rees, David, *Korea: The Limited War*. New York, St. Martin's Press, 1964.

Schlesinger, Arthur M., Jr., *A Thousand Days*. Boston, Houghton Mifflin Company, 1965. New York, A Fawcett Crest Book, 1967.

Sorenson, Theodore C., *Kennedy*. New York, Bantam, 1966.

Spanier, John, *American Foreign Policy Since World War II*. New York, Praeger, 1965.

Truman, Harry S., *Memoirs: Years of Trial and Hope,* Vol. II. New York, Signet, 1965.

Ulam, Adam B., *Expansion and Coexistence*. New York, Praeger, 1968.

United Nations, *Everyman's United Nations*. New York, United Nations, 1968.

Walton, Richard J., *The Remnants of Power: The Tragic Last Years of Adlai Stevenson*. New York, Coward-McCann, 1968.

Index

"The Cold War is a curious war, unique to our time. In a sense, it is well-named, for the two chief protagonists, the United States and Russia, have yet to engage each other in direct military conflict. But if the world has thus far avoided nuclear war with its unimaginable consequences, this Cold War has too often been hot. In Korea and Vietnam and in lesser conflicts men have died by the thousands. And the price has been not only death and injury but severe political, social, and economic dislocations the world over."

Why have both sides paid and continued to pay this price? Is it because, as some American statesmen have claimed, the Cold War is a moral struggle between Democracy and Communism, "good" and "evil," which can only end when one is victorious? Or is the United States more at fault for the hostilities, as "revisionist" historians have begun to say recently? Others wonder if blame can be fixed; perhaps each side, victimized by its own ideology, has tragically misinterpreted the other's motives, interests, actions.

Using an open-ended approach that encourages discussion, *America and the Cold War* does not attempt to reach any final conclusions. Instead, it offers the reader a coherent overview of recent history by presenting clearly, straightforwardly, what has